Victims, Villains and Heroes
Managing Emotions in the Workplace

What Readers Are Saying

Just finished reading *Victims, Villains and Heroes: Managing Emotions in the Workplace* and I need to tell you that you are right on the money. If business America would only read this book, we would have fewer problems in the workplace. Your insight in bringing the teachings of Loy Young and your own experience cannot help but ease the problems that individuals have, not only in the workplace, but also in their personal lives. Good work and my congratulations!

> *Ken Varga, President*
> *Professional Buyers Guild*

Victims, Villains and Heroes: Managing Emotions in the Workplace has contributed a valuable piece to my education in relationships, which are the core of my business (and yours!). The old dramas I used to unwittingly play took about 70% of my energy—energy that can now be used productively. I've learned how to avoid the hidden traps of the Victim, the Villain and the Negative Hero—the ones at work, and the ones battling it out inside of me. I've stopped trying to save the world and started taking care of me, and ironically—am making MORE of a difference now—and having more fun working and laughing a lot more. I am being my own Hero, and the satisfaction that comes with that is amazing. My effectiveness as a speaker, trainer and consultant has increased with this knowledge. I am becoming a much wiser woman! Loy and Don, much gratitude.

> *Bobbie Jones, trainer and consultant for IBM,*
> *Advanced Microdevices, Samsung and many US clients*

Excellent...excellent...I have just finished reading the new book *Victims, Villains and Heroes: Managing Emotions in the Workplace* ...congratulations to both Loy and Don!! Don made a statement that deeply touched me personally. He stated something about "owning 100% of the content, or 100% of the audience." This immediately reminded me of my own style of "teaching" and "counseling," which is to give sooo much information and want them to "get what I am wanting them to get" rather than what they are wanting to get out of it or letting them have their lessons...because I am afraid I will lose control. I'm going to recommend it to all my clients.

Rene Schulz
Schulz Associates
Business Consultant

I can't tell you enough how going to your seminar last week has impacted my life. The ideas you talked about, I have been repeating on a regular daily basis. The 80/20/40 image of managing energy has been particularly useful personally. And last but definitely not least, the parallels of using your ideas in my home life has been amazing! Without going into all the details, let's just say that my husband and I have actually been really communicating since the Friday seminar!

Anne Dor, Co-Founder
RM Automation Systems (Knowledge Acquisition, Assessment and Automated Verification)

Attending one of Don's seminars made the decision to buy this book an easy one. As a business consultant who deals with how HR impacts a business' bottom line, I found this book a veritable treasure trove of gems and nuggets of practical wisdom. His metaphor of "the stage" is pure genius and has yielded the unexpected bonus of benefiting my personal life as much as my professional. I would stake my reputation on recommending this book to anyone who has to manage people at the workplace, and fully expect his ideas to become universally accepted in the years to come.

Rick Neyman, Broker
Slaton Insurance Agency

Victims, Villains and Heroes
Managing Emotions in the Workplace

Don Phin
Loy Young

The Aquarius House Press
Escondido, California

First edition, 2002
Second edition, 2003
Third edition, 2004
Fourth edition, 2007

Publisher: The Aquarius House Press in cooperation with
DonPhin.com

Editors: Kathryn Hall and Karen Risch
Graphic Designer: Francine Dufour

Printed in the United States of America
10 9 8 7 6 5 4 3

Library of Congress Control Number: 2001095839

ISBN: 1-882888-63-4

Contact:
DonPhin.com
5713 Corporate Way, Suite 102
West Palm Beach, FL 33407
800-234-3304

don@DonPhin.com

www.DonPhin.com

The Aquarius House Press
PO Box 804

Escondido, CA 92033
877-704-4640 / 800-234-3304
www.AquariusHousePress.com

This book is dedicated to all the people who go
to work every day, at every type of business,
doing every type of job.

May the wisdom contained in it
help you eliminate destructive dramas
so you can have fun earning a living!

Foreword

Years ago, when I read Loy Young's book, *The Plot: Dealing with Feelings*, I was inspired to work closely with her as I went through the ending of a business partnership. Throughout the preceding years, I had been studying, learning and doing my best to apply the finest business relationship practices available, but it wasn't until I read this book that I began to unravel my own "plot" around business relationships. I discovered how deeply all of us are involved in *The Plot* we create to succeed in business.

Once we begin to discover the dimensions of *The Plot*, it becomes easier and easier to see others in it—and ultimately to catch ourselves in it. What a shock to see how attached we are to being victims, how much we want to be the hero to others but abandon ourselves to save them, and how easily we can become the villain when we feel hurt and wronged.

With this book, Don Phin has created a magnificent complement to Loy young's original work, and it takes the conversation about workplace woes and their solutions to an entirely new level. The distinctions in *Victims, Villains and Heroes: Managing Emotions in the Workplace* will forever make a difference in the way you relate with people in both personal and business relationships. I wish I'd had this information when I first began in business. Understanding *The Plot* has made such a difference in my life, in the lives of my partners and associates and no doubt will do the same for all those who read this book.

The power of this work was so obvious that we implemented the basic teaching in our business programs. Loy has been one of human relations favorite instructors at our Excellerated Business School for Entrepreneurs. This understanding supports and helps many to have more profitable relationships and thus make more money.

I met Don Phin, Loy's co-author, as a student in the **"Money and You"** program presented by Excellerated Business Schools. I was immediately struck by his focus, pragmatism, love and compassion. Don is the prototype of the new professional for the twenty-first century. He understands that his professional success, as well as the success of those around him, has as much to do with people's feelings as with his technical skills or anything else.

Don's unique ability to bridge various disciplines and take a common-sense approach toward workplace relationships is destined to make a significant contribution for years to come. We are blessed to have Don working with Loy to co-author *Victims, Villains and Heroes: Managing Emotions in the Workplace*.

This information is universal. Every human being, no matter what race, religion, background, gender or relationship status can benefit from this technology. This is about how we have a tendency to take up others' space and not allow them to express themselves, to be and to grow around us. This is about how we can shrink around certain energies and personalities and not express ourselves fully. This is about becoming a more powerful, clear and loving business person.

I wish you great success in feeling your way out of *The Plot*.

DC Cordova
Co-Founder
Excellerated Business Schools

Preface to the 4th Edition

Writing and publishing *Victims, Villains and Heroes* has been an incredible journey of discovery and understanding. The feedback to earlier editions of this book, as well as from workshop attendees, has been humbling and motivating. The private e-mails, post-workshop discussions and spontaneous "ahas" have brought with them an added sense of responsibility. As we teach, we don't feel responsibility *for* you, the reader, or *for* our clients and workshop attendees, but responsibility *to* everyone we reach. We're constantly cautious to remember that this material has to be about letting someone become his or her *own hero*.

In light of our practical experience, we have reorganized portions of the book with each edition, added some thoughts and exercises, and tightened up the text. Many thanks go to all of those who helped with previous editions and to Karen Risch for her great job of editing this one. We express much gratitude, especially, to all those who have encouraged us to continue this powerful work.

Here's to being your own hero and letting others do the same!

Don Phin and Loy Young

Contents

Foreword ix
Introduction 1

The World's Most Popular Plot 5

Part I ~ The Stars 9
    The Victim 11
    The Villain 35
    The Hero 47

Part II ~ The Drama of Work 63
    A Professional Performance 65
Part III ~ Becoming Your Own Hero 85
    Emotional Energy 87

Part IV ~ Workplace Heroes 127

Conclusion 145

Summary: How to Become Your Own Hero 147
Feeling Your Way Through the Plot 151
The Plot Poem 159
Also by Don Phin 160
Also by Loy Young 162

Introduction

"All the world's a stage
And all the men and women merely players.
They have their exits and their entrances
And one man in his time plays many parts"
                                        - As You Like It

Shakespeare's famous lines very aptly describe the emotional nature that fuels human action. All of us are actors in a never-ending drama. Our feelings thrive on drama, be it tragedy or comedy, is what our feelings thrive on.

Action, drama and stories give all of us what we need to learn from and to change emotionally. No amount of logic, facts or figures can ever change feelings, which is why reasoning rarely assists you in overcoming any problems of an emotional nature. You need to handle these issues on their own level. As Don often says in workshops, "If it doesn't make sense, don't try to make sense out of it!"

In writing this book, our goal is to give you powerful references to help you identify your emotions and their interplay with relationship scenarios surrounding you at work every day. This book isn't just about what you're *thinking* while at work. It's also about what you are *feeling* and how that affects what you think, do and accomplish.

Indeed, you'll learn how to be a more conscious participant in life, to deal with your feelings in a way that will make you proud and bring you peace. In this book, we'll share many of our clients' true stories with you to illustrate just how this works. To respect the privacy of people who have trusted us on their journeys, however, we have changed names, locations and other details that might divulge people's identities. To further ensure privacy, sometimes the characters in the stories are composites of several individuals.

The Play's The Thing

Have you ever sat at your desk, fantasizing about doing your job without having to work with or manage anyone else? Most everyone has. Have you ever heard yourself saying, "If people around here would only take some responsibility!"? Ah, this would makes sense, but where'd the *drama* be in that?

The game of work is being played on an emotional stage to an extent we are only beginning to understand. The task of your emotional nature is to express your feelings so others can identify the role you are playing. Whether at work or home, everyone acts out their emotional dramas using just three main character roles.

Emotions can keep someone playing the same old parts again and again like an aging ingénue who refuses to take on anything different. Often the scenarios are all too familiar, but as a person keeps finding a new cast, he or she remains unconscious of the parts being played and the characters assigned to others, even when that person should have outgrown a role long ago.

And so the book begins...

The World's Most Popular Plot

Goodness Triumphs Over Evil

People rave about and long to star in the popular emotional drama known as *Goodness Triumphs Over Evil*. Go back to the first written or spoken words, and you'll find this story carefully recorded time and again. Look at the Vedas, the Upanishads, the *Bhagavad Gita*, the Pali language spoken by the Buddha, the Bible, Egyptian hieroglyphs, the Koran, the writings of Confucius, Zoroastrian literature, even cave drawings. This play has been the hit show of the season for the last few millennia! And it's still running today.

But don't take our word for it. Have a good look at any blockbuster movie, popular television show, long-running Broadway play or best-selling novel right now—or from the last few centuries.

The struggle between good and evil girds the theme of any drama, even the ancient tales passed down orally in temples. Whatever the country, whatever the language, the most archaic and the most advanced teachings deal with warding off and defeating evil. This drama is what our emotional self lives for and is willing to die for.

The negative element is part and parcel of *Goodness Triumphs Over Evil* as it plays out in everyday lives. Hate and destruction are not exclusively in the domain of Hollywood fantasy. They take a real toll in world conflict, broken marriages, criminal acts and workplace dramas. The negative energy of this ancient theatrical school for our emotions fills our newspapers and courtrooms, and drives people to therapy sessions, drinking, drugs and ruin.

Life can resemble the movie *Groundhog Day*, starring Bill Murray, in which he repeats the same day over and over until he gets it right. Most people keep playing the same act again and again, and if the co-stars lose the zest to go on, there's always another performer waiting in the wings to take their places.

A certain script gets acted out every day and in every workplace. It parallels the emotional manner in which people deal with relationships. Whatever workplace you venture into, wherever two or more people get together, you will find the same plot being performed, whether it's in the sleek boardroom, by the water cooler or at the project management meeting. The stage may change, but the underlying drama remains the same. The second something feels "unfair," get ready for the performance to begin.

The Emotional Drama's Three Starring Roles

The script of *Goodness Triumphs Over Evil* features three starring roles: the **villain** who abuses and manipulates the victim, the **victim** who is powerless and looks to be saved by the hero and the **hero** who seeks to defeat the villain and save the day. Every person's emotions are always auditioning for one of these three roles. Remember, your emotional nature is like an actor whose objective is to express feelings.

Relationships are arguably people's favorite emotional game, and what motivates our true feelings is skillfully hidden from the scrutiny of the brain. Humans act out the play with their loved ones, with co-workers and even during time alone.

Through interaction with others, your whole range of feelings, from ecstasy to despair, gets to be expressed. How well you act out your feelings determines whether you end up with applause or egg all over your face. After the curtain comes down, however, *The Plot* gives you no rest, and you're hustled back on stage in no time at all.

This book puts a spotlight on the three roles all humans have mastered and play with others. You will become aware of your entire repertoire—and everyone else's. Although your emotions will keep you onstage, you may well want to choose your entrances and exits more carefully if you aim to be both happy and successful.

Part I ~

The Victim

Starring
The Victim

No Agatha Christie mystery, no John Grisham legal drama and no workplace conflict can do without a victim, the first star in *Goodness Triumphs Over Evil*. Ironically, this is by far the preferred role of our emotions, especially in a conflict, as it allows for the greatest drama. The pain, grief and suffering the victim endures can be so heart-wrenchingly and blood-drippingly dramatic.

Everyone has auditioned for this role many times in life; and no wonder. It's such a seductive role. The hurt and suffering victims endure usually elicit great tenderness. But there is a distinction between real victims and the victim mentality so prevalent today. If you get hit by a Mack truck, you certainly qualify as a real victim. No arguing that. But for purposes of this book, when we talk about the victim role, we are addressing the script you run and the behaviors you adopt to deal with the

Mack trucks in life. It's the part you choose to play long after the truck leaves the scene.

Taking on the mantle of victimhood, most people would rather blame somebody and throw themselves a "pity party" when things seem "unfair" than *take responsibility* and *do something about it!*

Usually people come to us for help after they've been devastated by a major crisis, such as being abandoned by a partner or getting fired from that ever-so-important job. Hardcore victims wait until misfortune strikes so many times that even they can't help noticing something must be wrong.

Most people need help with their feelings and relationships, as they were not taught relationship skills along with math or English. This difficulty is compounded at work because the control-based theory of personnel management that dominated the last century didn't factor in how people felt. However, dealing with feelings is a complex subject, and one not easily avoided. Its mastery can make all the difference in one's career and organization.

Portrait of a Victim

Victims need help. Overwhelmed by their circumstances, life appears to be far too complex for them to figure it out on their own.

By definition, no victim can have abundant resources — it would blow the role they know best:
victim. Nor can they sustain great relationships,
the ideal job, or any of the other achievements
most of us aspire to. In the end, they often gravitate back to the role.

Victims *can* eventually find a way to become their
own heroes, and it can take a long time. After all,
most everyone feels for the victim. This will often
enable continued victimhood.

If you are hooked on the emotional juice you get
from playing the victim role, don't be surprised if,
no matter what your mind says, your emotional
nature continues to seek out abusive people with
whom to play this part.

How can it be so enticing to keep returning to a
part you should outgrow? Here are some of the
feelings the victim role allows you to access:

Portrait of a Victim

vulnerable	emotional pain
powerless	hopeless
sad	rejected
low self-esteem	prone to illness
submissive	naive
anguished	fragile
fearful	dependent
suffering	depressed

Everyone experiences periods when they get to play the victim role — including at the workplace, and especially when things feel "unfair" or when they are new to a company or team.

In these rapidly changing times, people can begin many new professional endeavors in a lifetime. Anything new usually involves a learning curve. During this period, you can be like an infant and your emotions will have to learn how to crawl before you can run. Like a child, you can fall down. Many times as you move from the crawling to the walking stage. Eventually, you can run at a speed you like. You're especially vulnerable during the transition phase and need a lot of encouragement, even if it's from yourself.

During times of great change, you're wise to break things down and take them step by step so you don't feel overwhelmed. You must be willing to make mistakes without fear of judgment. What if you're managing someone who's going through this time of change? Focus on rewarding the effort, not the results. Once a person is encouraged, the results will come and in droves.

It is important to realize and remember that underneath all victims' pain lays a tenderness, a desire for sweet connection. This gentleness and sensuality make the victim role seem worthwhile. The big seduction of the victim role: *We finally get to feel ourselves!*

How can it be so enticing to keep returning to a part you should outgrow? Here are some of the feelings the victim role allows you to access:

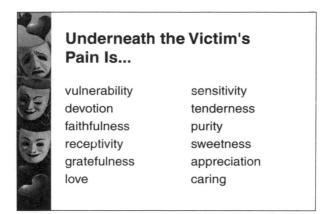

Underneath the Victim's Pain Is...

vulnerability	sensitivity
devotion	tenderness
faithfulness	purity
receptivity	sweetness
gratefulness	appreciation
love	caring

Every time a hero saves a victim, the victim's belief in goodness is strengthened. Life *is* fair! The victim is ready to audition for the role again, as soon as the curtain comes down after the final act.

Making a Victim

Hell has no fury like someone's emotional nature ignored. Our feelings are going to be the star of our own play, and everyone else's if possible, whether it's through sickness, tragedy or death if need be.

Many people do not like themselves enough to give their emotions the energy they need. They are *running so hard* that they fail to check in with themselves. Besides if they did, *they might not like what they feel*, so it's safer just to keep running, and we become disconnected. Eventually however, our emotions will get the attention they need, generally in the form of conflict with another person.

Where does this victim role come from? We need look no farther than our own upbringing. Have you forgotten how it felt to swoon over your high school sweetheart? The buckets you cried when he or she moved away? The agony of a math exam you didn't study for? The first time you rebelled against a parent's control? Do you remember? You probably do now that it's been brought up, but most people are so overwhelmed by the problems and worries of adult life that they forget the feelings of their youth, which often determine how they handle what comes up today.

The techniques acquired for dealing with upsets early in life usually determine the roles our emotional self chooses later on. That's why one of the most important questions we suggest you use in hiring, to really get to know someone is this: "Tell me something that felt unfair to you at your previous job." Then, when you get an answer, make sure to ask why, why and why again. When you get their answer, you'll know how they will deal with the inevitable circumstances that feel unfair to them working with you!

Here are some different types of victims and how their roles may affect them at work. Understand that each of these prototypes is an example on a broad spectrum. Each of us may have some, none, or all of these characteristics.

The Submissive Victim

Some parents can be domineering, accepting children only when they are quiet, sweet and demure.

As children mature in this situation, they often stay in the submissive role, speaking with the voice of a child and looking for authoritarian people so they can continue to receive acceptance in the familiar way.

Until these people grow up emotionally and learn to accept themselves, they will often *seek* or *attract* bosses, supervisors and other workplace relationships with authoritarian people who echo their domineering parents. They will often put up with harassing and abusive conduct instead of reporting it to management or anyone else who could assist in stopping it.

The Accident-Prone Victim Or Chronically Ill Victim

Some people are menaces to themselves and everyone around them. They stumble from one physical calamity to the next. For many, this has nothing to do with genetics. It happens because, as children, they were ignored unless they were the victim of an accident or some kind of illness. Then others would hear them scream and moan for help and rush to save them. Only when these victims learn to give themselves the attention they crave from others will they move past this conduct.

The Sexually Abused Victim

A startling number of the women who visited Loy for therapy and Don for filing a sexual harassment claim were abused when they were young. We have also worked with some men who were victimized at an early age. Most of these women and men kept their personal history secret until adulthood. Many of them closed down their emotions, at least their sensitive and caring emotions, as the consequence of the devastating experience in childhood. In most cases, consciously or not, they hated not only the relatives who robbed them of their positive energy but most members of the gender who abused them. The consequences in adulthood can be devastating.

How these victims reacted to workplace scenarios would differ dramatically. For example, one woman became an ardent feminist and had head-on collisions with each and every male authority figure in her life. Unfortunately, because of her overriding emotions, she filed a false claim of rape against four men, a rape that by all accounts did not occur. It was not until after deep therapy that she realized she had in fact fabricated the event.

Conversely, we have both helped women who did not know how to say no. Their self-esteem was so low that they could not bring themselves to hold the other person responsible for inappropriate conduct. Instead, they spent their time justifying it, often with excuses such as, "He's really not that bad," "I really need this job," "Hopefully, it will just go away," "Maybe I am overreacting," etc.

The *noise* in our heads, coming from the stories we developed in our past, can be a destructive force in our lives when not properly dealt with.

The Untouched Victim

There are some people who were never hugged or touched while growing up. To many of them, any touch has come to mean foreplay leading to sex. The mind knows the difference, but the emotional nature knows only what it feels. *We very often act on feelings, not on thoughts.*

For these people, personal space can be a real issue. For example, a friendly touch on the shoulder can quickly turn into an unwarranted sexual harassment claim.

Be aware that your feelings about personal space, how much you need and how much you give, may not be shared by your fellow employees.

The Battered Victim

One of the most common stage-setters for future victims is having alcoholic parents. Many children suffer brutal beatings that go unchecked and remain secret. Growing up, the only connection they know is through physical and emotional pain. That is intimacy to them, and so it's what they continue to seek as adults.

There are many adults who need punishment in one form or another to feel anything at all. And sometimes, self-punishment can be the most constant stimulus for feeling—and the most devastating. These victims often find themselves bouncing from one job to the next and eventually out of work altogether. Or they may regularly get hurt on the job and become incapable of working. Filing a disability claim is the ultimate proof of their victimhood.

The Learned Victim

We have all seen people who are born into a family or culture of victimhood. However, none of us has seen anybody maintain this emotional position and succeed with it over the long term.

The head of a nationwide organization for people with learning disabilities (herself disabled) told her audience that when things feel unfair at work, the first question should not be "What are my protections under disability law?" but rather "What are my responsibilities under these circumstances?"

Rather than looking to blame, she encourages everyone toward self-determination so that each person can become their own hero.

There will be people in every workplace who are *expecting* to be discriminated against or harassed. According to their story, it always occurs sooner or later, and due to the power of intention and attention, it is indeed bound to show up.

The best you can do is give these victims a different story to focus on, one of inclusion and respect, of challenge and opportunity, a story that can help them, too, become their own hero by taking responsibility, not by casting blame.

See No Evil, Speak No Evil, Hear No Evil

Working with a large number of victims, both chronic and temporary, we have found many interpretations of that role. But one characteristic is common to all: the perception of purity.

Many victims are innocent believers in goodness. No matter what the circumstances or situations, they never hear or see any evil. Because of their own naiveté, they would buy almost any story. They hang on the words of brilliant and colorful villains, taking every utterance as gospel while steadfastly ignoring behavior that belies those eloquent phrases.

Over and over, we have seen victims who were naive to the point of endangering themselves. These victims not only share all their secrets, but everyone else's as well. Victims give villains all the ammunition they need to abuse them later and when the inevitable happens, they persist in finding good intentions in whatever happens to them. They believe life was designed to be "fair" instead of the never-ending classroom that it is.

Many victims unconsciously encourage and manipulate situations so they can be believable victims. Forgiveness is a quality many victims develop along the way. However, forgiveness does not remedy the situation or bring *The Plot* to an end. Once the curtain comes down on the current catastrophe, the next plague of locusts is already on its way. The actors are granted only a brief breather before the victim emerges again, with ever more intense feelings.

For example, both of us have had clients with a preconceived idea of who their bosses, co-workers or partners were going to be. When they first met, they projected their stories onto the person and remained blind to much of reality throughout the relationship. They failed to realize that feelings, not facts, formed the basis of their relationships.

As a result, they would *ignore, bury* or flat out *deny* conduct considered by most to be unfair, abusive, discriminatory or harassing.

The victim's emotional nature trusts that in the end, no matter how long it takes, goodness will triumph over evil. One day the victim eventually triumphs over a perceived abuser and becomes a hero, even if only for a moment.

The Dark Side of the Victim

Playing the victim role has its dark side - as do all the roles we play.

The Dishonest Victim

Victims are usually too afraid to confront a person directly about a problem. Instead they will talk behind the person's back. The victim will long to expose someone else's inadequacies and make themselves feel good by comparison: "I may be bad, but let me tell you: He's ten times worse!"

The Irresponsible Victim

Everyone goes through a learning curve before mastering any subject. However, chronic victims refuse to participate in such an experience because they are too afraid of making a mistake and being rejected. This often happens in business relationships. For example, one partner may want to play it safe yet stands in awe of the other who is a real risk taker. He or she gladly lets the partner make all the mistakes and then cries "foul play" when anything goes wrong. They will deny any responsibility for the joint failure, claiming they were just following along.

The Compulsive Victim

Unless everything is in exactly the right place, compulsive victims feel out of control. And that's a terrifying feeling. So they compensate by being overbearing, while in reality they are just afraid. Being in control to the point of excess can be a solution to handling fear. However, if even one thing slips, controllers can feel like they are in a spin.

Both of us have seen executives who fit this role. While outwardly successful, fear runs their lives. As a result, they rule with an iron fist and hesitate to delegate anything. Being this kind of person in today's leadership paradigm, which is *the less I control, the more I will accomplish,* can be a terrifying reality. These executives are often "running for their lives" to mask their fears. They can destroy not only their businesses but also themselves and loved ones in the process.

Victims in the Workplace

The history of victimhood in the workplace has evolved rapidly over the last 100 years. Over this time the workplace has quickly moved from physical to mental to emotional priorities. For the first 25 years or so of the last century, concerns about health and safety claimed the majority of victims. You may be familiar with the Triangle Shirtwaist Fire of 1911, where sweatshop workers were forced either to leap to their deaths or get burned in their building because the owners had blocked all means of exit during the workday. Manufacturing environments existed throughout the country where children worked twelve-hour days, six days a week. Disease and physical injury were rampant in the factories during those years.

This period marked the beginning of modern workplace victimhood. Employees were cast as victims, and reporters and activists became the heroes as they sought to make villainous bosses abide by state-regulated health and safety laws. It was not until the passage of the Occupational

Safety and Health Act in 1938 that the country had a uniform standard for workplace health and safety.

Workplace victims in the second quarter of the last century focused on the struggle to speak and act with a collective voice that could negotiate for a better wage and job security. Mass strikes and protests crippled some of the country's largest businesses. The struggle spilled out into the street and involved heavy-handed law enforcement. In the end, union activists and legislators came to the rescue and gave employees the power of collective bargaining—a power that union representatives have used to the considerable benefit and detriment of the workforce over the years.

For the next quarter-century or so, the theme progressed past physical survival and became one of financial equality. Equal pay standards were demanded by women's groups. Minorities demanded equal access to jobs and other workplace opportunities. Particularly vulnerable during this time were people of color in the southern U.S. and those who had recently immigrated. When this conflict spilled out onto the streets, the legislators acted as heroes once again, passing the Equal Pay Act and the Civil Rights Act and coming to the rescue of workplace victims.

The last 25 years of the twentieth century took workplace victimhood to new and elaborate heights. As a result, employees now not only demand that they be treated equally, but that they treated "fairly." Crafty lawyers argue there is a covenant of "good faith and fair dealing" included in every employment relationship. They champion employees who "blow the whistle" or claim to have been victims of wrongful termination or worse, the intentional infliction of emotional distress.

Don began his law practice in 1983 while this paradigm was rapidly developing to its present state. After years of late night study, he couldn't wait to play the hero role. People came to his office in droves complaining they had been harassed, discriminated against, slandered or otherwise treated unfairly. They demanded justice and wanted to triumph over evil. And advocate he did, making it his life's mission at great expense to personal, family and financial well-being. (Ever read the John Grisham story *Civil Action?* That was Don.) He believed that if he did a really good job representing workplace victims, not only would he help save them from pain, he would also teach those dastardly villains a lesson and change their way of treating people. As it turned out, that's seldom what happened.

The Death of Control

For most of the last century, *The Plot* in the workplace revolved around the notion of control. Management told employees to do exactly what they were instructed to do. They would be graded on a scale from one to five. Those who survived until 65 would get a pension they would live off for two years until they died at 67 (anybody want that deal today?)

Then something changed: Overnight, a new understanding about control emerged. Suddenly, everyone woke up to the fact that control over people or things does not generate the profitability, security or ego gratification they so deeply desire.

Business leaders are now coming to an understanding that managing a workforce doesn't have to be equated with control or struggle. Today's workplace is more about how people *feel* than ever before. Millions of people are searching for *meaning* in their daily efforts. The good news is that in today's environment the opportunity for *becoming your own hero* has never been greater!

Managing Victimhood

In troubling times, it's critical to acknowledge the frustration, grief and pain (e.g., "It's OK to feel the way I do"). Try addressing your emotions physically, either by writing them down, by speaking into a mirror or walkin' and talkin' by yourself or with someone else. That allows you to get it "outside" of yourself. This is a critical step because *you can't begin to heal until you let go of your pain.*

Eventually, you can drill down and discover *why* you find yourself in difficult circumstances to begin with. What earlier experiences led to the beliefs and fears? What's the repeated conduct? Why does this seem so familiar? What's the lesson to learn?

Only then can you begin rebuilding your belief systems and learning your lessons so that you don't face similar circumstances in the future—so life doesn't become your personal *Groundhog Day*.

Just Do It

Victims are often plagued by depression. One of the best cures for this is physical activity. Don't think about what's getting you down for now. Just go to the gym, have lunch with friends, read a self-help book. Don't throw a pity party and wallow in your own misery—*do something!* Besides, nobody really wants to hear your worries if you won't do something to better yourself.

Begin by starting to move ahead physically and your emotions will catch up. Take small steps with low risk. As you gain confidence you will find yourself comfortable with bigger steps and greater risks. And remember, if you do take full responsibility, you need not get sucked into *The Plot*.

Victim Exercises

Realize that whenever you are stuck in the victim role, you may have cast others in the villain or hero roles. You may have a preconceived idea of who you want that other person to be, which could be different from who they really are.

1. Do you *really* know the people you work for and with? Are they *really* trustworthy? Or are you relying on an image of who you think they are or want them to be? Do these other people *really* know who you are? Or are you just a new character in an old play that began a long time ago? You'll know what the answer is if you hear yourself often saying, "They don't understand me."

2. Consider how your parents, bosses and other authority figures connected with you when you were a child. Do not bemoan how awful it might have been; just become conscious of victim scenarios you might still be acting out today. Then strive and triumph until you become your own hero. Former bad experiences you had will keep your emotional nature attracting similar situations and people to you, whether at home or at work, until you learn to become your own hero. And that's our emotional educational process. Each emotional scenario has "unfairness" embedded in it. One day you will triumph over the "unfairness"

and become a hero without hurting yourself or anyone else in the process.

3. Many people "run so hard" trying to keep up with the many responsibilities that they don't consciously create the time or space necessary to feed their emotional needs. Since emotions demand attention, even "successful" people will find themselves throwing a pity party or creating unnecessary drama in order to *feel something*.

   Have you stopped to check in with yourself lately? Do you even know how you feel? Or are you in fear that if you found out you would realize *"I don't feel so good"*? If that's the case, the solution is not to run right past the need to feel, the solution is to consciously stop and give your emotions the attention they deserve. Meditation, exercise, spiritual quests and heartfelt conversations can go a long way in preventing you from adopting the victim mentality - just so you can finally feel yourself.

4. To quote Joseph Campbell, the daily grind can be a "life-extinguishing affair." How can you bring a greater sense of meaning to the work you do every day? If you are an owner or manager, you may be all pumped up while the people working for you are dying on the vine — and you don't even realize it! How can you

help bring a greater sense of meaning or passion to the work they do every day?

5. As stated early on, one of the most important things a company can do is make sure that they do not hire a victim. One of the most powerful questions to ask in an interview setting is, "Tell me something in your last job that *felt unfair*." If they tell you "nothing," chances are good they're lying. If they tell you something felt unfair, do like kids do and ask why, why, why? Get to the root of the problem, and you will find their personality on full display. Then ask that question again and again until you have exhausted their entire job history.

What I Learned About the Victim Role or Mentality:

_____

_____

_____

_____

_____

_____

_____

_____

_____

_____

_____

_____

_____

_____

The Villain

**Starring
The Villain**

Since the days of Greek tragedies, the bad guys have always moved in the shadows: Scheming, cunning, cleverly plotting and doing whatever they pleased, they are undeterred by public opinion. Such power, determination, independence, mystery and danger are endowed with an undeniable sex appeal, with the promise of plenty of drama and the discovery of new, unknown terrain. As a result, the enemy often *charms* and *seduces* his or her victims into submission.

Playing the villain role can be fun! Goethe's Mephistopheles-devil is a rather more sparkling character than his comparatively pedestrian Faust-everyman. The devil has the expensive champagne-appeal, the *joie de vivre*. The role of the villain is therefore by no means despised in the *Goodness Triumphs Over Evil* show. This part demands more skill and depth of character than the rather staid good guys and girls who are victims and heroes.

Without a personification of evil, someone who consciously and intentionally harms the innocent and helpless, the show can't go on. The villain is a necessary character in our emotional education.

The Villain's Torture Chamber

Villains love to torture their victims. Over years of practice, the script has endowed the villain role with three characteristic tactics for bullying, intimidating and bulldozing people: *manipulation, control* and *abuse*.

Physical hurt seldom goes unnoticed, but to unveil a cleverly disguised villain, you must be able to *use your feelings*.

Your emotional self must feel when you are being teased or conned into submission. Your intuition must alert you when you are trapped in a gilded cage. Your emotions must recognize an abusive villain by the energy he or she emits.

The common denominator of all villains is a distinct *lack of heart*. They freeze you rather than cheer you. Their energy pulls you in quickly to take what they want from you rather than flowing outward to give generously—except when they're setting you up for a bigger take.

To detect the villain within yourself, you will need to remember a time when you enjoyed destroying something almost as fast as you built it. At that point, your heart connection closed and then you had feelings only in extreme situations. When this happens, your emotional nature always pulls you into horrendous dramas in which you can't help but feel eventually, albeit only the defeat and anguish of the victim role.

While you are in that vulnerable state, you can recover your heart by reconnecting with your feelings in the areas they went numb. Villains who change generally only do so through intense crisis scenarios.

A villain can be recognized by the following traits:

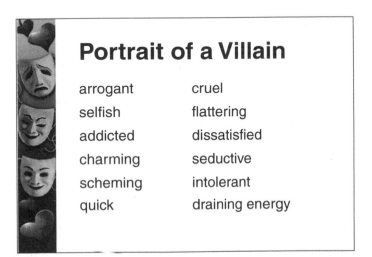

Portrait of a Villain

arrogant	cruel
selfish	flattering
addicted	dissatisfied
charming	seductive
scheming	intolerant
quick	draining energy

Victims rarely provide or experience fun in life. They stumble from one drama into another and need to be saved. The grief and pain never stops.

Meanwhile, heroes can be so consumed by their mission that they become way too serious. They set out to right the wrongs and save humanity, working around the clock and having no time for fun.

In stark contrast, playing the villain role can be fun and exciting—even if it is doomed to failure. Remember, goodness always triumphs over evil.

Making a Villain

Since the role of victim is a beginner's part and the hero's script a lot more demanding, there are many more victims than heroes in the workplace. Therefore, many a victim ends up screaming or praying for help while the heroes are busy elsewhere.

When a hero doesn't arrive, the victim's emotional nature experiences hurt, pain and betrayal. Life for the victim then feels unfair (e.g., "Nobody cares about me").

This unfairness can prompt the victim to detach from the pain and choose the part of the villain. The emotional self has identified the role of the victim as a dead end and decides to try a more promising role.

So the victim tells herself something like, "The part of the victim hurts too much. So I am going to model the only other role I know well, the villain! I know it may not last, but it's a lot more attractive than how I feel right now."

While playing her part and receiving the blows, the victim "stores up" the toxic emotions that have been aimed at her, especially the heated blasts she's taken from villains. She must get rid of these toxic emotions or suffer from them until she breaks down emotionally or physically. As a villain, she can hurl them at others, which gives her temporary relief from her emotional pain. To be on the safe side, the villain initially tests her strength by choosing victims who are weaker than she is and who cannot fight back (one common reason why children are abused).

Victims-turned-villains can find themselves hurting someone innocent or helpless without any apparent reason. Quite often, uncontrollable rages of anger go unchecked because they are surrounded by people too kind for their own good, who enable them and let them get away with their conduct whenever they feel like it.

These former victims' anger can be rooted in incidents forgotten long ago. They close their hearts so they can't feel the pain, which enables them to be insensitive and mean. They will search for any evidence to justify their anger, numbing out their memories so all that is left are their abusive actions, which can continue over many years, in different workplaces and homes.

We've All Played the Role

All of us have played the villain role. Have you ever yelled at someone when no emergency existed? Fact is, *yelling at someone is like vomiting on them.* (Pretty disgusting, isn't it?) Even though they may wipe it off, it stinks for a long time afterwards. As Stephen Covey would say, it "lowers the emotional bank account." In that moment of yelling, things felt so unfair that you closed off from your heart and hurled your "pain" at the other person— without caring about the pain it would cause them. Maybe because they didn't care about you and because you wanted them to *feel your pain*!

It is no different if that person is a five-year old kid who didn't clean up his or her room, the guy driving slowly in the fast lane or employees who made a mistake because they didn't follow (i.e., understand) your instructions. If you become accepting of yourself in this villain role, your heart can shut down permanently and with devastating consequences. You can become a true villain.

Even though villains often equate love with weakness, they can eventually learn to accept and begin loving themselves. Until then, they feel so much hurt from all the stored toxic emotions that they cannot empathize with anyone else and are mainly concerned with releasing their own pain.

The Rewards of Villainhood

But who says evil doesn't pay? Villains certainly can be quite happy with their rewards:

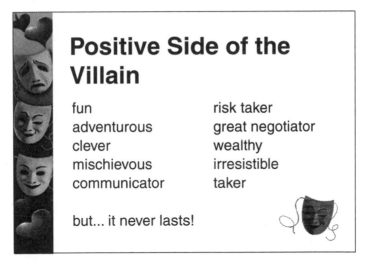

Positive Side of the Villain

fun	risk taker
adventurous	great negotiator
clever	wealthy
mischievous	irresistible
communicator	taker

but... it never lasts!

Obtaining these benefits without turning into a villain is an incredible challenge for all of us.

The Villain at Work

To quote JFK during a steelworkers' strike, "My father always told me that all businessmen were sons-of-bitches but I never believed it until now."

As the quote by JFK so aptly evidences, over the last one hundred years *management has been cast in the villain role* in most every movie, every book, every headline and every strike. (We challenge you to identify a movie or book to the contrary. And no, Ayn Rand doesn't count.) This is despite the fact that the vast majority of businesses and their executives create opportunities, produce jobs, put a roof over people's heads and food on their plates.

Many company owners and managers feel it is *they* who are being victimized. They feel the red tape and litigiousness surrounding the workforce relationship is so interfering that many of them do whatever they can, whether legally or otherwise, to shed themselves of responsibility for employee relations. Witness the growth of the employee leasing industry.

There is the common belief that only villains rise to the top and that to succeed means to compromise ethics and step on the less brazen or less fortunate. It is "they," the villains, who cause plant shut-downs, layoffs and wage cuts. It is "they," the villains, who seek to justify the pain they allegedly cause the workforce by pointing to the bottom line. Their "win" always comes as someone else's "loss".

This perception of *us versus them* continues its momentum as widening gaps in paychecks appear. Business lobbies hard to keep down wages, while executives make record incomes and layoff statistics continue at a record pace. Scandals like those surrounding Enron and WorldCom rock the very foundation of capitalism—and belief in corporate management. (A survey reported in the *Wall Street Journal* found 60 percent of employees believe management lacks integrity!)

As we continue to emphasize, no one has to work for villains or for anyone else. The decision to work for or with somebody else is a *choice* for which each person must take complete responsibility. While it may seem insensitive to point it out, we must: There were some Enron employees who diversified their portfolios. There were some Enron employees who bailed when their financial inquiries went unanswered. They protected themselves from Enron villains by taking 100 percent responsibility for their lives and careers, choosing to be their own heroes.

Villain Exercises

1. Have you ever been abused, controlled or manipulated by a villain personality at work? Did you ignore your inner voice that shouted "watch out!" Were you naive and surprised? How was this villain personality similar to someone from your past who took advantage of you and hurt you?

2. Are you dealing with any villains now? What harm can they cause? How do they react when others complain of their conduct? Are you afraid of speaking to them from the heart? Have you tried to get professional help to facilitate a conversation or protect yourself?

3. Identify examples of villains in the workplace. How often does the subject involve money, sex or power? Does their money, appeal or power ever last? Where do they eventually end up?

4. Can you remember a circumstance when you felt something was "unfair" at work and your response was to hurt back or harm another person? In other words, did you have a villain's emotional response? Which emotional tool of a villain did you use: abuse (physical or emotional), control or manipulation? At the time you may have felt justified in your response, but in hindsight, did you create unnecessary drama and harm?

5. Many of us won't attack others until we've become exhausted from beating ourselves up first. Be aware if you ever get to this point so your next hurtful activity isn't aimed at someone you care for or about.

6. Buckminster Fuller once stated, "Our greatest moment of integrity is when we realize we've made a mistake." When you realize you adopted a villain mentality and "unintentionally" hurt another person, you have a *moment of integrity* you can do something with. Begin with an apology and then make the commitment to *never* go there again! Realize the cumulative effect such conduct will have at work or at home and get the help you need to make a change for the better.

What I Learned About the Villain Role or Mentality:

_____

_____

_____

_____

_____

_____

_____

_____

_____

_____

_____

_____

_____

_____

The Hero

The star in every Western epic, every family saga, every Inc. 500 list and every Lawsuit victory is, of course, the hero. In the play *Goodness Triumphs Over Evil,* the hero takes the bullet but eventually rescues the victim from the villain's clutches. Both hero and victim know the script well. In the end, no matter how long it takes, goodness will triumph over evil!

Both victim and hero also know that the final act ends with the words *They Lived Happily Ever After.* Did you ever notice in the movies or on Broadway and in your favorite business magazine, that this ending scene is always very short and then the curtain comes down fast? We never get to see how the protagonists live happily ever after—if in fact they do.

Notwithstanding the brevity of the scene, both victim and hero know they will receive this magic energy, this happiness, just before the curtain comes down. It is their reward for having played their parts well. For example, Don will never forget the day a jury awarded his client a million-dollar verdict. (And, true to their roles as victim and hero, both Don and his client were broke three years later.)

This emotional high associated with the "triumph" prompts hero and victim to rush back as soon as the curtain comes down and audition one more time for the same roles in hot pursuit of vanquishing evil yet again.

Not many people have heard the term "hero mentality." But as with victims and villains there is a distinction between the hero mentality and a true hero. One is a myth and the other reality. The former can *cause* pain, suffer from compassion fatigue and eventually burn out. The latter, the true hero, is who we want to be.

Portrait of a Hero

Here are some of the qualities we develop by acting out the hero role:

Portrait of a Hero

powerful	determined
persevering	compassionate
caring	self-sacrificing
helpful	inspiring
responsible	giving
idealistic	disciplined
honest	humble
in control	

Making a Hero

As with the villain role, people often audition to be the hero after having tired of feeling like a victim. The difference is heroes *remain attached to the heart* and have finally found a method to save themselves, which becomes the solution for saving *other* victims going through similar problems. Every time the hero implements this strategy, *emotionally she relives saving herself.*

Triumph is the passion that drives the hero into action. The hero cannot endure the pain of seeing others suffer as he did in his role of victim, and he becomes intent on saving them.

There are people we work, live and play with who are fortunate enough to have been raised as a hero or to follow in a hero's footsteps. Some heroes champion the underprivileged or fight for a cause. Don and Loy went through such periods, and we continue to advocate for things we believe in.

Like the victim role and the villain role, the hero role has its destructive aspects. Often heroes begin to try to save others even before dealing with their own victim scenarios. The hate and negative energy these heroes can use to triumph over perceived abusers can be lethal.

Unfortunately, these "heroes" do nothing more than perpetuate hate, blame and anger. They file needless lawsuits, without so much as an attempt at negotiation. Hardball is their game. Eventually, the cause they are working on begins to get tainted and they collapse from exhaustion.

The purpose of the victim role is, of course, to play it over and over until you become your own hero. If someone else saves you, and you don't save yourself, you'll repeat the same scenario. Becoming your own hero is the final role in *The Plot*.

The Bored Hero

Most people can't imagine a life without conflict. Where's the drama in that? Wouldn't life be boring? Drama, albeit positive or negative seems to be required for our emotional natures.

A man came to Loy because he had just lost his third fortune. Earlier, his money had gone to ex-wives and children. This time, he had invested all of his funds in a bogus stock scheme.

As soon as the money was made, he found some way to get rid of it and then rushed back into battle to begin all over again. He didn't realize this behavior pattern until Loy helped him understand that emotions can't be argued with.

Making the money, overcoming adversity and struggling is how he fulfilled his emotional needs. He did not know how to *Live Happily Ever After*; being a hero was about conquering. To simply maintain wealth and happiness seemed a rather unexciting option in comparison.

Besides, most heroes don't keep money if they make any; it could tarnish their reputations. Just ask Robin Hood.

As we write about this gentleman, both of us are reminded of personal challenges we had to overcome when it came to money. Despite what our brains said, our emotions equated money with villainhood. With evil. With control. With scarcity. With becoming one of "them." Like many others, it wasn't until we "got it," that we got to make it and keep it!

The Three Stages of Hero Development

The person intent on living a hero lifestyle generally goes through three stages. In stage one, heroes begin to open their hearts by helping truly innocent or defenseless victims. These heroes often sacrifice themselves for victims, can be gullible, are often manipulated by villains disguised as victims, and frequently work for villains disguised as heroes. Many people find themselves in this spot just after finishing school and embarking on careers in the "real world."

The second stage of hero is the hero of strength, who with his/her devotion triumphs over the evil villain who is out front and obvious. Heroes of strength get their emotional energy to triumph from their ideals of "ridding the world of evil" or avenging victims. Social workers, nurses, police officers, firemen, nonprofit volunteers, lawyers and others who dedicate themselves to rescuing others fall into this category of heroes who often do so at their own expense.

The third stage of hero, a hero with a heart, is one who has developed her more sensitive feelings. After all, feelings are the language of the heart.

The hero with a heart uses the same script of *Goodness Triumphs Over Evil* to look inside herself, not just at the world. She discovers and saves the victim inside. She reveals and triumphs over her own harmful feelings and actions—the ones full of hurt, rejection, revenge and anger. With the hurt-victim energy and the harmful-villain energy dealt with inside, the hero with a heart will emerge. Only then can she deal effectively and consistently with villains in disguise.

Now the hero-with-a-heart's heightened sensitivity of feelings can distinguish between the real and the unreal. She can feel when she is being charmed, manipulated or controlled and does not often succumb with the gullibility of stage-one and stage-two heroes.

Heroes with a heart can now step up to their final role. They help others to take the same journey they have taken, to *become their own heroes* by saving the victim inside while triumphing over their harmful nature.

Eventually their hearts begin to beat with a creative passion that is joyous. No longer are they lured by the emotional drama of that tired old plot of *Goodness Triumphs Over Evil*. No longer are they bored without conflict, because conflict itself boring now. Their quest becomes learning to express the beauty they feel inside through their ideas, feelings, words, actions, relationships and vocation.

If they want drama, they will support a nonprofit cause, jump out of a plane, ride the rapids or go to a movie. They don't bring destructive dramas into their relationships at home or at work. They no longer wonder what's beyond that final curtain of "happily ever after" because they are experiencing it with every new expression of beauty in their own lives.

The Dark Side of the Hero Mentality

Heroes who demand that victims use *their* solution, instead of letting the victim find his or her own, end up being abandoned. Why? Each victim has to find a solution that works for him or her personally. We will not feel complete using someone else's solution, at least not for long.

Heroes often become over-controlling with their victims, which is unwarranted unless *there is a true emergency*! In an emergency, the hero may indeed need to take over and use every bit of strength possible to save the victim. While control is required to execute a good strategy in a crisis, too much control in a less extreme situation becomes repressive. An excess of heroic qualities can further violate the victim.

The hero is often horrible at listening. In their haste, they often pass over valuable insight and emotion. The other person feels this, and the fight or flight response is activated. The hero is often uncomfortable with silence and, as a result, can't benefit from its power. For example, the number one cause of medical malpractice is the failure to get a good medical history. The number one reason why a patient sues a doctors who has committed malpractice is his bedside manner. Go figure!

The following qualities in excess lead the hero and heroine to their dark sides:

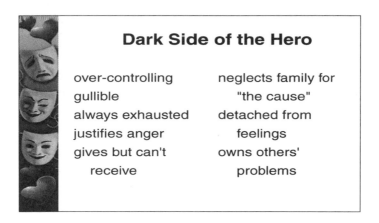

Dark Side of the Hero

over-controlling   neglects family for
gullible   "the cause"
always exhausted   detached from
justifies anger   feelings
gives but can't   owns others'
receive   problems

The Hero at Work

Traditionally, our culture has looked at three groups of people as workplace heroes. At first there were the union leaders. Remember the powerful scenes in *On The Waterfront* with Marlon Brando and *Norma Rae* with Sally Field?

Then came the legislators and the lawyers. They helped generate and enforce so many personnel laws that today's business owners have great difficulty in complying with what author Walter Olson refers to as "The Excuse Factory."

In recent times, enlightened business owners have been regarded as heroes. Herb Kelleher, Anita Roddick, Richard Branson, Paul Hawken and Jack Stack come to mind. They implemented employee-friendly workplaces before it was fashionable or legally required to do so.

Since the Erin Brockovich movie and the Enron scandal, the corporate whistle blower has also emerged as a workplace hero.

Now it's your turn to be a hero! Many people reading this book are in an ownership or management position, or at least hoping to be there some day. If that's you, you have a profound opportunity.

One of the most difficult tasks for any business owner or manager is to empower employees without controlling them. Unfortunately, too many owners or managers end up "owning" subordinate's problems, falling into the trap of being responsible *for* other adults, not just *to* them.

The victims' "I don't know what to do, so you have to help me" statement triggers a powerful emotional response. Heroes often find themselves coming to the rescue, doing the subordinate's job for them or punishing them instead of simply teaching them how to do it themselves. In the end, their managerial effectiveness has been gobbled up by "gotta minutes."

Ever seen a case where someone never seems to "get it" and has found a boss who will always come to the rescue? This is a classic example of a gullible hero (the boss) being manipulated by a villain *disguised* as a victim (the employee), the proverbial wolf in sheep's clothing. (Kids are great at manipulating parents like this.)

Heroes have difficulty sensing the con because they are so intent on saving someone. Yet you can tell a villain disguised as a victim from a true victim because nothing ever seems to work for villains disguised as victims. You can offer them solutions and show them how to fix the situation whenever they cry, but none of the solutions ever work because they're not trying. However, there's always a justification. Heroes with a heart can learn not to go for this manipulation.

One of the biggest challenges management faces with *The Plot* is that these three roles keep you working according to the Pareto Principle, which contends you spend most of your time and energy on the 20 percent of the workforce that produces 80 percent of the headaches. Because the victim role draws all of the attention, the heroes of the workforce, who produce 80 percent of the results, are often ignored. And we wonder why they leave us.

Unless acknowledged and supported, sooner or later the heroes in your organization will feel emotionally drained and move on to a new environment searching for fulfillment and recognition. Usually, they will leave without making a single complaint. On rare occasion, they may take an even more destructive route and start playing the villain or victim role.

It is admittedly difficult to break past limitations imposed by *The Plot*. Everyone falls into familiar patterns. One way to break out of these patterns is to *play social scientist* and experiment with different approaches to managing. For example, if you have difficulty with victim employees who do not take responsibility, instead of coming to their rescue, demand they come up with solutions to their problems, and then you will give them feedback. Teach them how to fish instead of continually throwing the fish at them.

When the employee asks "Can you help me with this?" Tell him you would be willing to do so, but only after he has documented his efforts first. Then don't settle for his first response. If his response doesn't give evidence that he "gets it," send him back to the drawing board. Sooner or later he will realize he can't manipulate you with expressions of victimhood.

One last note about the hero at work. It doesn't take much to push the hero to their dark side if they, or people they care about, are treated unfairly. Injustice or unfairness are "proofs" of evil, which cause emotional energy to start building in anticipation of conflict and ultimate victory.

We have to be careful not to transition into villainous activity when something unfair happens to us. In the face of injustice, we can be seduced into believing the end justifies the means. It certainly makes for an action-packed day as our emotional self plays its role in *Goodness Triumphs Over Evil*.

Hero Exercises

1. Do you like helping people and find yourself doing it at work? If so, are you allowing others to become their *own hero* or are you too busy trying to do that for them?

2. Who have been your heroes in the workplace? Did you ever have a boss who led by empowerment rather than control? How do you try to emulate this conduct?

3. Identify a time at work where you tried to help someone out but despite your efforts they never "got it." Were you dealing with someone who wanted to remain in a victim role? Did they take action or only justify why things wouldn't work? Did you have difficulty letting go of this person's problems because you cared so much about them?

4. Being your own hero at work is about the willingness to take 100% responsibility for your career. How would you rate yourself? If you're not happy with your answer, you might want to reflect on what ways you have not been your own hero. Do you need coaching from a professional? If you don't feel you need help, then what could you do to move more toward being 100% responsible for yourself?

5. Joseph Campbell stated in *The Power of Myth*, "A hero is someone who has given his or her

life to something bigger than oneself." The role implies personal sacrifice. It is important to distinguish between the myth and the reality. Is the sacrifice truly justified? Is there a real emergency or one of your own making? For example, a surprising number of arson crimes have been committed by volunteer firefighters. (What good is being a volunteer firefighter if there's no fire to put out?) Are you creating unjustified fires simply to play a hero role?

6. There are occasions where the "adventure" can bring forth latent hero qualities. The experience of Hans Solo in *Star Wars* is a classic example. If you are an owner or manager, in what way have you created such an "adventure" for your workforce? Some well-known examples of companies that have tapped into this power are Southwest Airlines, Nike, and Pike's Place Market (chronicled in *Fish Philosophy*). Is your company next?

7. Go to www.heromachine.com and build your own super-hero. Have everyone at your company do it and post the results in the hallway.

What I Learned About the Hero Role or Mentality:

_____

_____

_____

_____

_____

_____

_____

_____

_____

_____

_____

_____

_____

_____

Part II
The Drama of Work

A Professional
Performance

The Plot is a thriller. Traps open unexpectedly, doors
close behind us, curtains blow in darkened rooms,
the villain's rumors abound, blood-chilling realiza-
tions keep us up at night, fear drives us and the
victim starts to gather evidence. Where is the hero?
Stuck in a board meeting, helping out a struggling
co-worker, busy defending another victim in the
courtroom?

While our favorite script features three characters—victim, villain and hero—a riveting drama
really requires only two. The hero role is optional;
however, without at least a victim and a villain,
we can't stage a performance.

No matter how many people are on stage during a
confrontation, every single one of them will immediately clamor to impersonate the victim. No
weapon wards off an attack as effectively as
accusing someone else of foul play. You can choose
to use logic to argue your way into the victim role
or to express your suffering and pain emotionally—both approaches work.

The Arsenal

In many a performance of *Goodness Triumphs Over Evil*, people collect "emotional toxins" when they feel abused or belittled and don't defend themselves. The feelings of pain, grief, betrayal, rejection, anger and hate become lodged in the body and are unleashed to do battle with any real or imagined threat.

However, before the fight, the victims and heroes on stage need evidence of the crime the villain is blamed for. Once the proof is established, they feel justified in dumping their poison on the identified evildoers, be they co-workers, a boss or an entire company.

One highly effective strategy in a conflict, therefore, is to *convict our adversary of lying*. The minute we have sound evidence that he or she is a liar, the lethal battle with the villain begins.

Convicting the Liar

The truth, the whole truth and nothing but the truth. Every actor in our thriller swears to it. The villain knows that he is lying while he does so, but victims and heroes sincerely believe that honesty is the highest virtue of them all.

However, they often delude themselves and thus their actions do not match their claims. Victims, for instance, are cowards and, when caught between a rock and a hard place, lie to protect themselves.

Heroes admit frankly any mistake they have made—as required by their role—yet they will fabricate smooth and flowery lies without any qualms to avoid hurting another person.

One of the greatest traps of the hero is over-commitment. They say "yes" to make the other person feel good, even if their plates are full. When they eventually fail to live up to even a trivial commitment, the bond of trust is broken, unfairness emerges and *The Plot* thickens. Remember, the lies, even if generated by over-commitment, are never weighed against your other actions.

Finally, villains lie in order to abuse, control or manipulate.

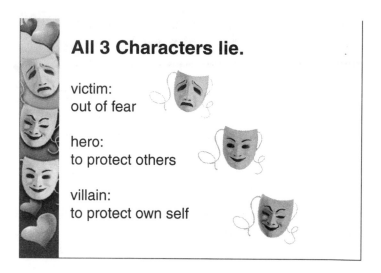

All 3 Characters lie.

victim:
out of fear

hero:
to protect others

villain:
to protect own self

Although all victims, villains and heroes lie as part of the script, a convicted liar is immediately condemned as a villain. The trick is not to get caught.

However, since everyone plays to win according to their role in our highly competitive workplace drama, some people constantly put their boss or fellow co-workers through the lie detector test.

The minute the liar is convicted, every player on stage instantly has permission to triumph over the "villain." Everything else a person has been or done in the past is forgotten the moment he is proven a liar. Remember, "no good deed goes unpunished." We even have jury instructions that embody this belief. As a litigation attorney, much of Don's job was to catch people lying, which casts them as villains in the eyes of the judge and jury.

Good lawyers are expert at this. What's more, they usually know a villain when they meet one. Given their experience, they are not as easily conned as the average person.

The California Jury Instructions below do a great job of explaining how to view the truthfulness of anyone, not just somebody on the stand. In closing argument, Don would read these instructions to the jury and compare it to the testimony offered by the witnesses at trial. Some of Don's notes follow in brackets and italics:

Jury Instruction No. 2.20

BELIEVABILITY OF WITNESS

You are the sole and exclusive judges of the believability of the witnesses and the weight to be given the testimony of each witness. [*An important point to remember. Ultimately, YOU are the one responsible for not getting conned.*]

In determining the believability of a witness you may consider any matter that has a tendency in reason to prove or disprove the truthfulness of the testimony of the witness, including but not limited to the following:

The demeanor and manner of the witness while testifying; [*I would tune in to their body language, eye movements, breathing, tonation, pace and so on to detect dishonesty.*]

The character and quality of that testimony; [*What facts, documents and witnesses do you have to corroborate your testimony?*]

The extent of the capacity of the witness to perceive, to recollect, or to communicate any matter about which the witness testified; [*Liars are fond of saying "I don't remember". One of my favorite questions to ask, "Well, when do you think you forgot? A week afterwards? A month? After the first meeting with your attorney?" Of course, the opposing attorney would object to that last question but the point was already made.*]

The opportunity of the witness to perceive any matter about which the witness has testified; [*Primarily time and place issues. Brings to mind the cross examination of the "eye witness" to the robbery in* My Cousin Vinny. *Turns out the witness's eyesight was so bad she couldn't see a few feet away, never mind across the street.*]

The existence or nonexistence of a bias, interest, or other motive; [*"He's my brother," "I needed the money," and so on.*]

A statement previously made by the witness that is consistent or inconsistent with the testimony of the witness; [*See the more detailed instruction on this below.*]

The existence or nonexistence of any fact testified to by the witness; [*As Lincoln proved using the Framer's Almanac- there was no moonlight that night.*]

The attitude of the witness toward this action or toward the giving of testimony; [*The refusal to answer the tough questions.*]

An admission by the witness of untruthfulness. [*For example, they told another witness it was a lie. Usually saved for impeachment purposes on cross-examination.*]

The character of the witness for honesty or truthfulness, or their opposites. [*"He doesn't have an honest bone in his body. Just look at all the other times he's been sued, the five aliases and criminal record."*]

The witness' prior conviction of a felony. [*Keep in mind how high the rate of recidivism is and do background checks.*]

Jury Instruction No. 2.21

DISCREPANCIES IN TESTIMONY

Discrepancies in a witness's testimony or between such witness's testimony and that of other witnesses, if there were any, do not necessarily mean that any such witness should be discredited. Failure of recollection is common. Innocent misrecollection is not uncommon. Two persons witnessing an incident or a transaction often will see or hear it differently. Whether a discrepancy pertains to an important matter or only to something trivial should be considered by you. [*I would always search for inconsistency in recollection. If someone didn't remember, I could then go to "recorded recollection" and introduce a police report, memo, etc. to see if it would revive their memory.*]

Jury Instruction No. 2.22

WITNESS WILLFULLY FALSE

A witness false in one part of his or her testimony is to be distrusted in others. You may reject the entire testimony of a witness who willfully has testified falsely on a material point, unless, from all the evidence, you believe that the probability of truth favors his or her testimony in other particulars. [*Once someone gets caught in a lie they are guaranteed to be villainized!*] This is one of my favorite instructions!

So, before you take the bait, consider how you or the other person would stand up to this level of scrutiny.

Getting Out of Conflict

Nobody wants to be play-acting alone. (Where's the drama in that?) When people at work come at you with their dramas, don't get sucked in—*it's a trap*! After years of experimenting with different approaches, Don suggests using the mantra, *"Wow, that's interesting!"* Or, you might want to shorten it and say to yourself, "Far out!" "It's a trap!" "What would Jesus do" or "What would Scooby-Doo? Whatever works best for you.

By practicing this first step you will be able to step back for a moment and separate yourself from an immediate emotional override. (P.S. This also applies to the dramas that take place during your self talk.)

Scientists are discovering a direct link between how long we hold on to a hurtful event and the long-term damage it can cause. As we relive an episode, neurotransmitters are sent out that further engrave the episode in our mind, and our body, eventually incorporating it into our "story."

Whether the unfairness is real or perceived, the bottom line is the same. We must detach and do what makes sense. If we don't we'll find ourselves rushing to the victim role, or worse, turn into a villain, if even for a moment.

Now that you have stayed off the stage, the next step is to get out of the playhouse altogether. If you're in a particularly challenging relationship at work, tell this co-worker, supervisor, partner, or CEO that you won't participate in a conflict with them. Let him or her know you will sit down or take a walk and resolve your differences, but you won't engage with them in combat. If necessary, you will leave long enough for the addictive, competitive energy to dissipate. Someone has to stop the war, and it's going to be you.

It is best to negotiate your agreements long before a fight begins, when the atmosphere is cool and calm. Otherwise, you will be defeated before the battle starts. If your boss says, "I demand that you stay when I'm yelling," inform him that you are taking your guns and cannons off the battlefield. You will retreat even if he considers you a coward, but when the smoke clears, you will be back.

Once you step back, ask yourself "What else could this mean?" If your boss is a good person deep down, while you are gone she will begin to regret her villainous conduct. If she is a true villain, she won't care how you feel. If that's the case, find a new boss!

If you are facing someone who is out of control, you are facing a villain who feels justified in harming you. Simply excuse yourself and walk away. Immediately. Then get some help from a counselor, lawyer, coach, religious leader, police officer or respected friend.

If you do not want to be a victim, then do not take any abuse. None. Nada. No más! It's that simple.

You do not have to take abuse, and you do not have to engage in battle to prove you are strong.

Become the hero or heroine by getting out of the line of fire.

Take a walk if you're too emotionally charged up and breathe in through your nose and exhale through your mouth. Walk and breathe, walk and breathe: that's the way of the inner hero. Breathing and walking pulls you out of your angry mode faster than anything else. Do not come back until both of you have cooled off.

Avoiding Conflict

Disengage: Say, "Wow, that's interesting!" or walk away

Find a safe release of feelings: journal, walk, breathe, etc.

Repeat: "We are both good people"

Ask: "What could this mean?"

This step sounds so easy—and yet is so difficult to take. You'll have to face the fact that your refusal to engage in combat may upset the other person.

Now he is left with all this energy worked up and nobody to dump it on. If he doesn't release it somewhere else, the aggression will eventually make him feel worse about himself.

That's the real victory, letting the other person feel bad about himself for his harmful feelings and actions. As we said, the greatest point of personal integrity is when we realize that we've made a mistake. Only when you "get it" that you can hurt others, will you change your ways.

And here's a wonderful treasure you'll begin to find: Trust in yourself. You'll feel confident you can get yourself out of a conflict and avoid injuring people emotionally.

Walking off the battlefield without engaging in combat or shooting a single bullet with your words is much tougher than fighting—especially when you've got evidence that the other person is the villain this time and you could win. But the streetwise hero is above medals, war decorations, courtroom victories and "being right."

Resolving Differences

Now that you've disengaged, it's time to deal with your feelings. There are times when it is wise to sit down and write about the hurt you feel. You can also talk to yourself in the mirror or engage in dialogue with a trusted friend or advisor. You'll probably discover it's a hurt you've had for quite some time that drags you back into *The Plot*, tempting you with the role of villain. We can assure you that if you do hurt someone with your anger, you will only drive yourself deeper into *The Plot*.

To resolve differences, you really have to *want* a solution—which means you must be prepared to listen and compromise. You must believe that *you and the other person are both good people*, able to find a solution that works for both of us. Remember, very often what comes to you comes *from* you.

Note: This does not mean you have to be naive in dealing with others. Blind faith is for the foolhardy. *Checks and balances* are mandatory when it comes to trusting people.

Again, try to negotiate your agreements long before the drama begins, when the atmosphere is cool and calm. In Aikido, the participants know that a slap on the mat means the opponent has suffered enough pain and it must stop. "Time out" is a phrase used in many a combative sport. What time-out mechanism can you agree on in advance? Remember, the hero's game is not playing "win/ lose," but rather getting matters of the heart resolved with a "win/win" solution.

Keeping Away the Predators

Let's say you are being approached at the workplace by someone in whom you have no romantic interest. First you must deal with yourself. How are you feeling? What emotions are you being flooded with? Are you crystal clear about what is happening here? Have you disengaged, so you can think clearly?

Then, how will you deal with that person? How will you prevent yourself from turning into a victim or villain and causing unnecessary pain?

Be attuned to the potential for drama. What is your intuition telling you? For instance, is this person you are dealing with being overly flirtatious? Is he or she having problems on the home front? Offering to do things for you that he or she does not do for other employees? If you are dealing with someone who is being overly flirtatious, you will need to mention your wife, husband, boyfriend or girlfriend in any discussions (make one up if you need to). Make it very clear to the person that this is where your interests lie. This type of approach keeps you from heightening the drama. You do not need to say, "You don't interest me" for starters, as it will put that person on the defense.

If he or she is having problems at home, think twice about becoming the shoulder he or she cries on, no matter how important it might make you feel. It could easily lead you into feeling sorry for the person, and not wanting to be unkind, you might get yourself into a compromising situation. Avoid casting yourself as the victim in a sexual harassment drama.

Handling the Serious Villain

As a hero, it is your job not only to save victims but also to triumph over villains. However, you must

know your capabilities. Serious villains are dangerous, and you don't want to engage with them if
you are a beginning hero. So get help.

As long as you are playing *Goodness Triumphs Over
Evil*, a violent confrontation is won by physical
strength (might makes right) or mental and emotional power. If you are attacking the villain with
outer force only, and are out of control emotionally,
the villain will use your own strength against you.
Whatever you do, disengage your energy from the
villain as soon as you can. Do not let him thrive on
your energy—force him to live off of his own,
which will drive him crazy.

As you shall soon see, exposing the villain's true
role is also part of becoming a hero. You may have
to "blow the whistle," file a grievance, send an
anonymous note or fire somebody. As long as the
villain remains hidden, you and others are subject
to his destructive ways.

Handling the serious villain often requires professional help. Don't hesitate to call an attorney,
psychiatrist or law enforcement officer if need be.
Becoming your own hero does not mean you must
do it alone.

The Rewards

What do you gain by playing your role year after
year with a few extra props, a touched-up back-

drop and a new cast? What keeps you suffering, makes you cry buckets or strands you in the emergency room at the hospital with a heart attack? How is it you find yourself testifying in either the victim or villain role in the courtroom? What holds you glued to the bottle or the drugs, enduring and struggling, until you overcome adversity? Wouldn't life bore you to tears without any drama?

You suspect every other person on stage of plotting your downfall. You are constantly on red alert to engage in a fight the moment you perceive any trace of unfairness, dishonesty, manipulation or abuse in another person.

Why don't you just have a ball in the final act of *They Live Happily Ever After* and leave it at that? Do you really need the pain? Can't you just have fun? There must be some spectacular benefits for you to keep running back to play the same tired script over and over again—and there are!

The Plot is your emotional education system. It is the primary form of relationship training in life, including in the workplace. The victim role is the easiest part, and the one everybody begins with. You must graduate to either the villain or the hero part; otherwise, you may well find yourself run over or fired for being the victim.

The trial and error approach to personifying the villain or hero eventually teaches you power and cleverness, which are important factors for your survival and personal growth.

In the end, the show leads you to your vulnerability, to yourself. The ultimate character role of the show is the inner hero, which requires a great deal of self-actualization and maturity.

The drama guides you, not too gently, to finally conquer the inner villain and save your inner victim. Unless you create peace and balance between your inner victim, villain and hero, you will be plagued by inner turmoil and continue to seek external conflict with others.

Once you accept and respect all your roles, you don't have to depend on others for your moments of happiness. You can truly be joyful and live your own version of happily ever after.

Workplace Exercises

Countless people emerge from disappointing workplace relationships without trying to find the negative aspects of these relationships within themselves.

How would things change if you interpreted the facts in your story differently? Perhaps if you viewed your struggles as learning opportunities?

You discover these by asking yourself the following questions:

1. In what ways do I feel like a victim at work?

2. What characteristics does the villain have that I feel powerless to deal with in a way that I'd be proud of?

3. Once you have the characteristics written down, examine past experience to discover if you've exhibited the same characteristics with someone else.

4. If you do not have compassion for the other person's character defects, chances are it's because you have the same characteristics inside of you.

5. How well do you know your own story? If you are like most people, you have spent years of your life watching and reading about other people's stories. Now it's time to write your

own. Spend a quiet hour and write a five-page story about you and work. Then step back, take a look at it and understand that it is this story, whether accurate or not, that governs much of your emotions and conduct in the workplace. How would things change if you interpreted the facts in your story differently? Perhaps, if you viewed your struggles as challenges or learning opportunities?

If you become your own hero, you no longer have to perform the victim role. You'll no longer attract villains into your life. You'll be ready to graduate from the emotional education system of *Goodness Triumphs Over Evil.* You do not graduate by just becoming a hero and saving others. There are far too many victims to save, so your job will never be done. Life will continue to be unfair.

It's only when you become a hero to yourself that you become free of *The Plot.*

What I Learned About the Drama of Work:

_____

_____

_____

_____

_____

_____

_____

_____

_____

_____

_____

_____

_____

Part III ~
Becoming Your Own Hero

Emotional Energy

Most everyone we work with has a lot of experience acting out all three roles of victim, villain and hero, both in the workplace and at home. Heck, we've had that experience, too! (Like we said, *nobody* escapes this journey.)

However, the concept of *being one's own hero* can sometimes make people feel lonely or frustrated. If you have to save yourself, then that means no one cares enough about you to do it on your behalf. After all, if you're innocent, pure and sweet, shouldn't a hero come to save you? Perhaps a mentor or guru will show up. At least that's how the story is supposed to go.

Yet there comes a point—after you've called for help way too many times and there just aren't enough heroes to go around—that you decide to save yourself by becoming your own hero. As Zig Ziglar says, "If it's to be, it's up to me!"

If you're courageous enough to step out of the drama we call *The Plot* and experience a new story in which co-heroes reign, an essential part of the solution is an understanding of what we call *emotional energy*.

Your emotional energy is about how you feel, not about how you think. Human emotional energy

developed thousands of generations before consciousness ever did. The fact is, any time the
emotional energy is out of balance in a relationship, it will cause unnecessary, subconsciously
driven, destructive dramas. Mastering how you
use your emotional energy can create significant
breakthroughs in your career—and life.

Let's pretend you walk onto the emotional stage by
yourself. How much of the emotional energy
would you own on it? This is not a trick question.
You would be right if you said 100 percent.

Now let's pretend you are on the emotional stage
with another person. Let's say you want to have a
good relationship with this person because you
either work or live with her. This person may be a
co-worker, boss, subordinate, spouse, child, parent—you name it. We'll assume you prefer the
hero role and want to treat this person fairly. In
that case, how much of the emotional energy
would it feel right to take up on the stage now? If
you are like most people your answer would be 50
percent. That's the response we receive during
workshops all around the country.

However, when was the last time you were at 50/
50 on any stage? Depending on the stage you are
on, you generally have the weaker or stronger
energy which usually isn't an issue until the
second something feels "unfair".

For example, you may have a weaker energy with a boss and the stronger energy with a subordinate. You may have the weaker energy with a parent and the stronger energy with a child. And so on.

To simplify matters, let's call people with a weak energy on the emotional stage "20 percenters." It should come as no surprise that when you play with a 20 percent energy you gravitate toward the victim role.

Let's refer to people with a strong energy on the emotional stage as "80 percenters." When you play with a strong energy, you typically play either a hero or villain role. Once again, the difference is villains have become detached from their hearts. *They don't care* in that moment.

Relating With 20 Percent Energy

When more than one person adopts a victim mentality, and therefore each takes up only 20 percent of the available space, there's too much space between to be heart connected. As a result, little is likely to get accom-
plished. Because of control-based management practices and low self-esteem, many workplaces are literally made up of 20 percenters. (Just ask Dilbert and his crew.)

While it is helpful to talk about these different energy levels, it is even more important to *feel* their differences.

Try this exercise that we use in our workshops with one of your friends or a group of people.

Begin by pretending you're standing on a small football field and that the space represents 100 percent of the emotional energy available. You can experience what a 20/20 relationship feels like by having half of the group line up on one 20 yard line and the other half on the other 20 yard line. For most people this feels *very distant*. We are emotionally disconnected. It's hard to make a heart connection with people who take up only 20 percent of the space, since they usually aren't present enough to reciprocate.

Remember, nature abhors a vacuum. When you play as a 20 percenter you will attract someone who is an 80 percenter to take up the rest of the space—either heroes who they hope will save them or villains who are quick to abuse them.

We've all seen what we refer to as 20/20 couples. They're the ones who sit on the couch every night staring at the television, throwing a pity party and blaming everyone else for the condition they find themselves in. Sometimes you just want to grab them by the shoulders, shake them and tell them to *go do something about it* and quit moping.

If you own or manage a company, it wouldn't be surprising if you have felt this way a time ... or two ... or three... or...

Emotional Steamrollers

Now let's pretend that as you stand across from each other, one of you decides not to play the victim role any longer and wants to start *doing something*. Remember, when people no longer want to remain in the victim role, they gravitate either toward a villain role or a hero role.

Let's say you are a young man growing up in a poor neighborhood. Chances are not too many heroes are running around. Chances are many of the people *doing something* are engaged in villain-ous activities (e.g., dealing drugs, committing crimes). So you detach from your heart and begin engaging in criminal activity. If someone were to confront you and say, "Don't you realize that statistically within the next five years you will be dead or in jail?" You would most likely respond with something like, "What else am I supposed to do around here?" When you are reminded that the drugs you sell hurt other people, your response will most likely be, "Why should I care? *Nobody ever cared about me!*"

Remember, if people don't feel cared for, they can turn villainous and justify harmful activity. Just ask the employee who files a frivolous lawsuit or after a reprimand tries to rob your company blind.

All of us have adopted the villain mentality at one time or another. All of us have yelled at someone else in non-emergency situations. In that moment *we didn't care* if we hurt the other person. We didn't care about their feelings because *we felt they didn't care about ours.*

For purposes of this book, we are going to presume that most of the time when you act with strong energy, you are doing so for what you believe are good reasons. You remain attached to your heart and you do care. So you start running. You are doing it. You are getting somewhere. Eventually, you get your career advancement, or your business grows, and material success follows. Life is good. And now you are ready to help others.

Now let's go back to our exercise. This time, let's pretend one side of the field has decided to start doing things and adopt a hero mentality. They begin running. (Have one side run in place.) As a result, they get a measure of outer success. Seeing this success, and in search of a hero, the remaining victims raise their hands and yell, "Help!"

What does any good hero do under the circumstances? Of course, he or she comes to the rescue. (Isn't it true that the other person doesn't even need to ask for help? Often the hero cares so much help is already on the way.)

This time, when the 20 percenter says "help," have the 80 percenter run right up to the victim's toes and say, "I'm here to save you."

Chances are this immediately feels uncomfortable (and probably will lead to a number of chuckles and laughs as well). How does it feel physically to the 20 percenters? Probably too close for comfort. What are the options when someone is in their physical space like this? Answer: fight or flight. Every time. There really are no other alternatives. As Loy says, we resort to our animal natures. (The antelope doesn't wait to have a conversation with the cheetah. It feels *the vibe* and splits!)

The point to grasp here is this: *the same thing goes on when you enter into a person's emotional space. You may not be able to see it, but they sure can feel it!*

Often the 20 percenter feels steamrolled, which usually brings an end to heart-based relating. The 20 percent person now closes his heart or runs away so he doesn't get hurt again. Alternately, he may try to push you back so he can be his own hero. Again, the fight or flight response.

The 80/20 relationship is the nature of co-dependency. When people rush to play the hero role, they cross over the line into the victim's emotional space, whether invited there or not. Then, despite "good intent," the other person either shuts down or tries to prove them wrong. It happens every time.

That is why the greatest challenge for heroes is *staying on their side of the line*. Especially when they "care so much." Unless there's a clear emergency, stepping over the 50 percent line and invading someone else's emotional space will eventually cause you to be perceived as an aggressor, controller and villain.

This is true *even if your intentions are good!* You see, the emotions only *feel* and will cast you into your "default role." If you are a boss, salesperson, or parent, you will surely be cast in the villain role because that's how the story goes.

If you habitually take up more than your 50 percent of the space, like an 80 percenter does, the only people you will consistently get to work with will be 20 percenters. That's the only kind of person there's room for.

Note: It is a dangerous position for any business owner or manager to surround themselves with 20 percenters! These 20 percent people usually become co-dependent on them. Most likely, 20 percenters will not be able to tell the 80 percenters what they are thinking and will talk about them behind their backs. That is why so many CEOs are the last ones to learn the truth.

Eighty-percent people may say they want to be around others more like themselves, but there is no room for other strong people in their lives.

An 80 percent person is not necessarily contentious by nature. A lot of exciting people who are great communicators can just be overly strong and take up too much emotional space. *Intense* would be one way to describe the habitual 80 percent person.

Eighty-percenters often get rejected as other people try to kick them back into their own fair share of emotional space. If that doesn't work, they try abandonment as another recourse, leaving in order to find enough space to breathe. Fight or flight, every time.

What causes people to go over the line and take up too much emotional space in the first place?

Instead of feeling their fears and cautiously walking through them, they run for their lives, trying to get past their feelings. At 80 percent, they're moving so fast the speed numbs out feelings so they no longer feel fear. They are so strong that they do not feel their own or others' hearts, either.

In the end, anything over 50 percent is destructive unless there is an emergency. Assess your own life to see if this isn't true. Can you see the harm you've caused in relationships at work or at home when you've been at 80 percent? That's why we also call this position the *Negative Hero*.

You can begin to alter this simply by observing your conduct. People who want to be heroes usually are willing to change once they truly come face to face with the harm they've caused, even if it was unintentional. Only villains like to hurt others with all their justifications.

Relating with 80/80 Energy

What happens when two 80 percent people get together? We won't ask you to demonstrate this one. It's like the helmets colliding on *Monday Night Football*. There just isn't enough space for 80 percenters to relate to each other except through conflict, sparring with each other to see who will back down. This is one reason why many litigators (who are predominately 80 percenters) have a hard time negotiating settlements in workplace disputes. They tend to attempt negotiation while they are invading the other party's "safe zone." If you are ever in litigation, try to get to mediation fast!

If you find yourself in an 80/80 situation, get off the stage and seek out a strong mediator who can push people back to their "side of the line."

The Joy of 40%

While playing 50/50 may sound right, there's a practical problem in actually taking up that much space.

Let's once again go back to our exercise. Now walk toward each other to the middle, which represents 50 percent.

Face each other, leaving no space in between. If you're like most people, you'll feel crowded and uncomfortable as you practically stand on top of the other person. Notice the word *feel*: feelings are

50% the language of the heart— and the key to sensing your personal space.

In workshops, Don will kid and ask, "If my wife and I are trying to plan our vacation from a 50/50 energy, where are we going?" Most workshop participants will be quick to respond, "Nowhere!" (Every once in a while a wise guy will say, "Anywhere she wants to go. If that's the case, it was an 80/20 decision and if it turns out bad, it's her fault.") The fact is, when you play at 50/50 you smack one agenda right up against another. There isn't enough "safe space" to co-create a solution.

Now that you've experienced what it feels like to be at 50 percent, begin to step back if you haven't already. Don't go too far back, just to where you feel comfortable. For most people it is an arm's distance. You are now standing at your "40 percent" line.

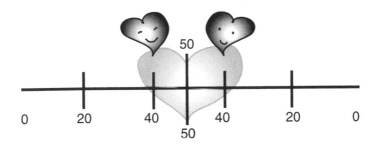

This *feels safe*. Yet you are still close enough to connect. The room in the middle is for the dance, for where you figure it out together. It makes co-creation possible. It allows us to laugh. And it's the only thing that works emotionally. By playing 40/40, everyone on your team and in your home can become their own heroes.

When you think about it, a tuning fork works off the 40/40 principle. Too close, no sound. Too far, no sound. Just right: vibrational harmony.

Moving From 20 to 40 Percent

As a leader, how will you get victims to show up emotionally? How do you break past their *culture of silence*? One way is to create an emotional attachment to positive actions. In a sense, we want to catch people doing something "right." For example, if your concern is about the willingness to speak up about inappropriate conduct, you can publicize the experience of a worker who took personal responsibility and used the system with good results. That person may act as a mentor and encourage other similarly situated employees.

Likewise, one reason why most employees don't contribute to company suggestion systems is that they do not feel it is *safe* to do so. The 20 percenter fears a lack of acknowledgment or, even worse, ridicule and rejection. To overcome these fears, a company can place pictures and testimonial notes next to the suggestion box, which provide emotional encouragement. Even better, your company should *require* that employees come up with suggestions as part of their job description. When they do, *reward the effort, not the result*. That comes later as the quality of suggestions improve with time.

If you are not relating to others in this fashion, then just what are you doing? Trying to control them? Trying to use your solution to save them and exhausting yourself in the process?

People who habitually operate at 20 percent don't have enough self-acceptance to take up more emotional space, and that's why it's important to express from your heart what you genuinely like about them. You can give them energy by helping them *feel good about themselves*. You can do that by *finding the good in them*.

Acknowledgment (which is really about acceptance) is the greatest form of encouragement for a 20 percenter. If you do not invade their emotional space, people begin to feel safe with you and are more likely to come out emotionally.

But if you go into their space, they will feel you are too strong for them and may retreat even more, often looking for another job or relationship without even letting you know what happened or why. As a result, you will never have the opportunity to engage in the deeper level of communication with them.

It does little good to tell 20 percent people what's wrong with them. Chances are they already know what it is. Since they're already in a victim state, they are very sensitive to rejection, so feeling more rejected will only drive them further back—one reason why poor performance evaluations seldom improve performance.

All of us are 20 percenters at different times during our lives. Infants are certainly at 20 percent or less while learning how to operate their bodies. Also, any time you start something new, you're vulnerable as you go through the learning curve. It takes a while for you to develop your self-confidence and move to your 40 percent in a brand-new endeavor. That's natural.

This is one reason why we suggest companies use an employee survey after someone has been with the company for 60 days. (See the "HR That Works 60 Day New Employee Survey"). It conditions new employees to come out of the shadows and speak up. What's more, their "outsider" perspective can be an extremely valuable source of insight and innovation.

One Step at a Time

When helping others move to 40 percent, encourage them to take one step at a time and focus on the effort, not the results. (These will come later and in droves.) The same thing goes for when you are on that journey.

Being a 20 percent person means having lots of fears. Someone in this position should list the fears and then understand that fear is not a red light. It's a yellow light saying move ahead, but cautiously.

Learning how to speak for yourself is an important part of moving to 40 percent. A Toastmaster's class can work wonders. So can giving a lunchtime talk to co-workers.

Fear is the oldest and deepest of all emotions. You can get through your fears by being connected in the moment. Fear is usually about an imagined, not an actual future, which keeps you from moving forward. FEAR is said to stand for False Expectations Appearing Real. When you worry about an imagined, fear-filled future, this fixation often acts as an emotional magnet to draw the feared experience to you. But if you just keep moving ahead

slowly, when you get to the future you'll find it
wasn't as scary as you expected.

The ability to *coax, encourage* and *inspire* yourself
and others emotionally is perhaps the most powerful tool in your personal and business arsenal. So
just how do we get there?

One of the best first steps on the journey toward
40 percent in any area is an education. Education
allows us to know where to take the first step.
That is why *education is the greatest form of leverage.*
For example, Don had to go through an emotional
journey related to money. In Don's emotional story,
money was identified as the root of all evil. Robin
Hood didn't keep any, and neither did Don. It
could have tainted the hero image.

Of course, none of this made any logical sense. For
example, Don knew plenty of wealthy people who
did wonderful things with their riches. They were
heroes in every sense of the word. But again, the
emotions laugh at any logic.

As an example of Don's victim mentality when it
came to money, he would never read a book such
as *Think and Grow Rich,* simply because of its title.

Once Don got clear about how destructive his
story was with money, he began to read everything
he could about money. He read every book on how
to be a millionaire and every book on how to be a
successful business person. This allowed him to

take the first steps toward financial and business success. Ten years later, he now has both.

Where do you, your workforce, clients or customers play with a victim mentality? Where do they have a weak energy? Do they know where the first step is? How can you coax them to take a first step through education? Simply say, "Let's try this and see how it *feels*." Can you think of a safer statement than that?

Once you are educated as to where to take the first step, you must go ahead and take the step. But what is the fear of the 20 percenter at that point? Most people would respond "making a mistake" or "the fear of failure." And they would be correct. But what are the emotions behind these fears of failure?

The answer to that question is perhaps one of the most insightful parts of this work: The fear of failure is directly related to the judgment of the 80 percenter in your story, on that stage, someplace. For example, going back to Don's emotional story about money, the judgment would have been of the collective "us" he grew up with. Financial success would be the emotional equivalent of selling out. Struggling and conquering was the emotional story Don knew all too well.

If this is the case, who is the 80 percenter on the emotional stage where you or another feels like a victim?

Let us share a story that points out how *this dynamic escapes no one.* On a plane ride from New York to San Diego, Don sat down in the aisle seat. Sitting in the window seat was a gentleman who looked like he walked off the pages of *Forbes* magazine: Armani suit, Bally loafers, $200 hair cut. He looked like the epitome of success. When Don sat down, he gave a heartfelt hello as always, only to get a grunt for a response. Don said to himself, "I got it, you're important; I will leave you alone and do my work."

To Don's surprise, about an hour into the flight the executive (who we will call Tom) spoke up and said, "So what do you do?" Surprised even to hear from the fellow, Don replied, "I just finished giving a workshop to CEOs about the drama of the workplace." In response, Tom expressed interest and began questioning Don continuously for close to an hour. Their exchange then went something like this:

Don: "Tom, before you go any further, let me take a wild guess and ask you a question. My sense is that you are dealing with a lot of drama at work and a lot of drama at home. Am I right?"

Tom: "You are weird. [Pause] How did you know that?"

Don: "I could sense it. So tell me, what is the stage that you find yourself on? What is your business and home life like?"

Tom: "I live in a $3 million house in Greenwich, Connecticut, run an advertising firm on Park Avenue with fifty employees, have three daughters in the most expensive private school in Connecticut, two golf club memberships, I drive the latest Mercedes, and my wife doesn't have to work."

Don: "Sounds like the all-American dream to me. So, what do you want to do? Chuck it all and train elephants?"

Working with many CEOs over the years, Don is well aware of what it feels like to be trapped in a "gilded cage." The 80 percenter can create a great deal of material success and then end up being trapped by it. As they say, they've climbed to the top of the ladder only to realize it's leaning against the wrong wall! But now they are stuck and have to continue running for their lives to maintain their lifestyle. And guess what? It doesn't feel fair!

Don: "Seriously, what would you like to do?"

Tom: "I would really like to go back to me and three employees. I love the advertising business. Problem is that I don't get to do it any more. Seems like all I get to do is manage fifty personalities every day. I'm simply not enjoying it any longer."

Don: "It seems pretty clear to me that if you want to go back to the work that you truly enjoy, you will have to simplify your lifestyle. Let me ask you this, do you think you could move into a $1 million dollar house and eliminate your mortgage payments altogether?"

Tom: "I would have no problem with that. I find that I have to talk to my wife and daughters through the intercom most of the time as it is."

Don: "Would you be concerned about the judgment of any of your neighbors or colleagues if you made such a move?"

Tom: "No, I would not."

Don: "I take it from our discussion that you probably have very little time to use those two golf club memberships. Would you have any trouble selling those?"

Tom: "No, I wouldn't. You are right: I don't get to use them. And no, I'm not concerned about what the members would think."

Don: "Do you think it could be possible to take your daughters out of the most expensive private school and perhaps put them into a less expensive private school or even one of the Greenwich public schools?"

Tom: "Funny thing is that I have been talking to my wife about this. I am concerned that my daughters are being protected from a socialization process that is invaluable. I went to New York City public schools and probably benefited in my career more from the socialization skills that I learned than anything academically. I've seen too many kids come into our business who have been gated throughout their entire lives, and now as young adults, seem to have completely detached from any sense of reality. And no, I would not be concerned about anyone's judgment on this including that of my wife or my children!"

Don: "Did you have to trade in your old Mercedes for the new one, or could you have simply kept driving the one you had?"

Tom: "What, are you following me around? No, I could have kept the old one just fine, and I wouldn't have the ridiculous lease payments I do now."

Don: "What about your wife?"

Tom: [before Don could finish what he was about to say] "She can work"!

Don: "So, what I am hearing from you is that you can take all of these steps that would be necessary to recapture joy in your career, but what I haven't heard is *whose judgment you are concerned about*. In my experience, people feel like victims, and are in fear of making a change, or as they say 'moving their cheese,' because of somebody's judgment about them. Who's the person in your story whose judgment you would be concerned about if you

tried to recapture the joy of your work and some-
how failed in the process?"

At this point and time Don could see Tom really
digging in. There was a period of reflection and
then a significant change in his facial expression
and breathing pattern.

Don: "You just got it, didn't you? Who is it?"

Tom: "My dad."

Don: "Now we are getting some place. I'm very
familiar with that story, too. What did the old man
ever say to you that encouraged you to build this
gilded cage that you now find yourself trying to
escape from?"

Tom: "I'll never forget the day he told me *I would
be a failure in business!*"

In the book "The Four Agreements" Don Miguel
Ruiz states that one of the ancient agreements is to
be "impeccable with our word." This is precisely
what he means: It is important to understand that
what we tell people can stay with them for a
lifetime! Whether they are a partner, co-worker,
subordinate or a child. Tom's father may have said
many wonderful things to him, but Tom had
latched onto the negative judgment. Be very
careful of what you say to people when you adopt
a villain mentality, even if for only a moment. As in

Tom's case, it could affect their story for the next 30 years.

Don: "Have you ever tried to have the 40/40 discussion with your father? Having done that myself last year for the first time in my lifetime, I can tell you that it is a powerful experience."

Tom: "I can't."

Don: "Sure you can."

Tom: "No, I really can't."

Don: "Why not?"

Tom: "Because he has been dead for five years."

As you can see from this story, no one escapes *The Plot*. Everyone has a place, whether at work or at home where they sometimes feel like a victim. If you are to become your own hero and live the life you truly desire, you are going to have to not only educate yourselves and take action, you are also going to have to be very clear whose judgment can get in your way. Even if it's your own!

For many people, especially 80 percenters, nobody places more judgment on them than they do themselves! If this is you, instead of dealing with your fears, you run right past them. If there are any setbacks along the way, you will beat yourself up harder than anyone else would dare.

Chances are others won't call you on your "stuff" because they feel your energy and don't want to mess with it. As a result they end up becoming enablers.

Moving From 80 to 40

In workshops, Don asks participants, "What is the fear most 80 percenters have about moving down to 40 percent?" The answer is almost uniformly "the loss of control." Yet the ability to let go of control is the 80 percenters' liberation. Again, this is because *the less you control, the more you will accomplish.*

Eighty-percenters moving toward 40 percent need to begin thinking in terms of *including others* as opposed to *controlling* them. Becoming *inclusive* is the mantra for the 80 percenter. If you do anything that affects someone else, you should get their input. After all, you need their support, and unless you include them in the process, your plans will be sabotaged. There's a new way to work with people and it's called *Management by Agreement.* (Isn't that how you want to be managed?)

In many cases, just being aware of this alternate perspective helps you to move back. However, you will need to uncover feelings you decided long ago you didn't want to feel. Why? It was partly because of their suppression that you went out to 80 percent in the first place.

On the way to becoming an 80 percent person, you usually developed wonderful rules for how to live life. These rules were your solutions for all the fears you wanted to outrun. Now you often try to convert others to these rules because you want everyone to be like you, and you think these rules will make you safe—but they won't.

At a workshop, one CEO with tears in his eyes said he "got it." He said he was too strong with his son. He realized why his son batted better when he was sitting in the dugout as opposed to when he was coaching on the third base line. He realized that his son's concern about his judgment heightened when he was in view and it negatively affected his swing.

This a powerful insight and a great metaphor. How is your energy affecting the "swing" of the people in your workplace? Has their performance suffered because they fear your energy? Do they feel safe around you? If not, chances are you'll seldom get the chance to laugh together or engage in a second level (deeper) conversation with them.

Conversely, whose judgment is affecting your swing? Is it real or imagined? Have you addressed your concern with them?

P.S. This metaphor applies equally well both at work and at home.

40/40 Leadership

The Oscar - winning movie, *A Beautiful Mind*, chronicled the life of Nobel Prize winning physicist John Nash, who taught that we did not have to adopt the win/lose thinking fueled by the likes of Darwin, Marx, Malthus and Smith in order to prosper. Nash showed empirically how win/win systems produced greater abundance than win/ lose systems do. The "Nash Equilibrium" is reached when a system is created such that when everyone plays by the rules, everybody benefits. When somebody violates one of those rules, they can't prosper as a result. The application of the Nash Equilibrium to work financial systems may be Nash's greatest legacy.

When you think about it, the Nash Equilibrium sounds a lot like playing 40/40. In the book, *Good to Great*, author Jim Collins details the factors of hyper-successful corporations. He concluded that they are led by the "humble" executive. From our perspective, this is the executive who plays 40/40. Collins shows how among executives who are 80 percenters, such as Lee Iacocca of Chrysler fame can burn out and then leave a vacuum behind when they move on.

It is important for CEOs, managers, supervisors, teachers, salespersons, and parents to understand that when you cross over the line, it is hard for the other person to distinguish your energy. While you may be trying to act as a hero, *it feels no different* than if your energy was villainous. Because our emotions are governed by the stories we tell ourselves, this is a dangerous position to find yourself in: You will be cast in the villain role. Again, unless there is a true emergency, there is no justification in going over the line.

The Law of Attraction

Like Don did, many 80 percenters harbor the belief that success is the result of struggle, sacrifice, and running harder than the next guy. If that's how you learned to survive, it can have devastating effects on your life balance and eventually career or business. Giving up control can be a scary proposition to say the least. But what Don and many others have discovered on the journey from 80 percent to 40 percent amazing things takes place—the Law of Attraction begins to kick in.

For the first time you find yourself wading into the Sea of Abundance. Prosperity and happiness *come to you*. Struggle disappears and potentiality is limitless. A new spirituality awakens inside.

You have to trust us on this one, but ask yourself this: How could it be otherwise? If you believe the universe is abundant how could you possibly attract its energy as a 20 or 80 percenter? Only at 40 percent are you in balance with the universe around you.

Speaking for Yourself

Listening is one of the rarest talents. Many people hear, but few listen. However, to be heard and listened to is a basic human need—as much as food and drink are. Without the fulfillment of that need, humans are incapable of a normal social interaction.

To be heard, you need to learn how to speak from your heart. Then people will feel safe enough to be attentive to what you say. Not only that, when you listen as a 40 percenter you can begin to *feel* what the other person is saying.

The emotional guideline for speaking from your heart is always to speak about yourself, then others can hear. In contrast, when you speak about the other person, they usually stop listening and start reacting from an emotional place.

Here are words to use when speaking for yourself:

I think...

I feel...

I did...

I said...

I noticed...

My experience is...

My actions were...

My perception is...

Heroes DO NOT speak for the other person by saying:

You think...

You feel...

You did...

You said...

Your experience is...

Your actions were...

Your perception is...

Use language that keeps the conversation on your side of the line. The minute one person begins a sentence with *you,* he can cross that line and start to put the other person in an emotionally defensive position. That person will generate fight or flight feelings *without even realizing it!*

Audio reception turns off whenever the emotional nature prepares itself for battle. If you sense this happening, you've just activated the story of *Goodness Triumphs Over Evil* one more time. Regardless of the circumstances, the other person feels like an innocent victim, and you've become a person who is harming them emotionally. Time to start gathering the evidence to accuse you of villainous behavior!

Be especially careful using the *you*-word while disciplining somebody at work. It is better to say, "I notice it's 9:20," than to say, "You are late again!" While both statements are accurate, and deliver the same message of dissatisfaction, one does so while keeping you on your side of the line. You *focus on the conduct, not the person.* By doing so, you are not placing the other person in a position where they could quickly turn you or themselves into a villain. You avoid the unnecessary drama.

If followed properly, this approach will bridge differences and avoid conflicts. Once you begin to set the example of speaking from your feelings, other people's emotional natures will soon follow.

You, You, You!

Okay, let's say you've really worked at speaking from your own experience with *I, me,* and *my,* yet someone in your life at work or home always hurls *you* at you. What do you do? You need to get them speaking about their own experiences instead of yours. *How* is the question.

Here is a sample script to be spoken with an accepting tone of voice that expresses, "You are a good person." Please use your own words—this is just a sample script.

Remember, you are educating someone who probably never learned about heartfelt communication skills as you did:

> *Please, I need to speak for myself, When anyone says 'you this' or 'you that' to me, I inevitably become defensive. It would be most helpful to me if I was told about your feelings and experiences and allowed to speak for my own. Is that okay?*

Summary

Arriving at 40 percent can be a lifetime's journey, but it is well worth the effort. Playing at a 40 percent level means you are in balance with your *beingness* and your *doingness*. It means you are 100 percent responsible for your personal conduct, and you do not play blame or justification games.

When you arrive at 40 percent, success comes more naturally. Little of your energy is wasted on distracting and destructive dramas. You end up being more effective in less time, growing in your career, making more money and having more fun in the process.

So, play a 40/40 game!

1. The oldest story of them all is *The Plot*, which always requires at least a victim and a villain. It is the age-old story of *Goodness Triumphs Over Evil*. Any time people cross the line in an effort to "triumph," they unleash a destructive emotional energy.

2. People are generally the 80 or 20 percenter in a relationship. A true hero is a 40 percenter, as this position allows room for growth and creativity within the relationship. The 80 percenter can *include* others' feelings, whereas 20 percenters can step up and start *doing something* for themselves.

3. One of the greatest challenges for people who believe in personal growth and want to do

good toward others is not becoming a "negative hero." Regardless of good intent, you have to stay on your side of the line. The only time it is acceptable to cross over that line is in an emergency (e.g., someone is literally drowning or hurting someone who is defenseless). A true hero can best help others if they *coax, encourage* and *inspire* them to action. The challenge is to allow the victim to find the hero within. *It is their journey, not yours.*

4. If somebody wants to get you on stage with them, don't accept. Say, "Wow, that's interesting!" Stay off the stage and avoid the drama.

5. If you are an employee and your workplace is one big dysfunctional *Plot*, don't get caught up in the drama. Seek help from a professional if need be, but don't allow yourself to be controlled, manipulated or abused. There's no need, just as there is no need to stay in an abusive relationship. If eliminating *The Plot* from your own thoughts and actions does not allow you to thrive in your work environment, we repeat—find a new one.

6. And last, being a 40 percenter is about understanding your feelings. You won't change until you understand the nature of the pain, frustration and conditioning driving your circumstances. When you finally let go of that, play a 40/40 game, and take 100 percent responsibility for becoming your own hero, you will have graduated from *The Plot!*

What I Learned About Using My Emotional Energy:

_____

_____

_____

_____

_____

_____

_____

_____

_____

_____

_____

_____

_____

_____

_____

Exercise: Assessing Your Emotional Presence

One of the most powerful questions you can ask yourself is "How am I feeling?" Get a sense of "What feels unfair?" or "What's driving me crazy?" Then ask yourself, is that the feeling of a victim, villain or hero?

These questions have a number of aspects to them, some or all of which should be considered.

Environment

- ❏ How does your working environment feel?

- ❏ Is it intimidating to you?

- ❏ Is it intimidating to others? .

- ❏ Is there a way to make your surroundings feel safer and more inviting?

- ❏ Is there a place you can go to that would feel safer and more inviting?

Body Language

With a 20 percent person, you want to use your hands to coax, encourage and inspire them up to 40 percent. You can beckon the person closer with your hands. Likewise, when someone is at 80 percent, you can gesture with your hands in such a way as to say stop, so you can begin to speak. Otherwise, you might be in for a long monologue. At 40 percent, your body language is inclusive, open and inviting. You use your hands to include others. You are also aware that standing can be threatening and suggestive of 80 percent energy, especially around a 20 percent person.

Tone of Voice

Our tone of voice usually accurately expresses our feelings. If you have a little girl or little boy voice, then you're more likely closer to 20 percent. If your tone of voice expresses urgency or little feeling except perhaps for some anger, then you've moved past your 50 percent toward the 80 percent mark. A 40 percent voice is slower with a full tone, yet not overwhelming.

Speaking

❑ In a conversation with someone, do both of you express yourselves an equal amount of the time (40 percent)?

❑ Or do you speak far too little and rarely contribute your own ideas (20 percent)?

❑ Conversely, do you monopolize the conversation (80 percent)?

Eye Contact

Being at 40 percent means making eye contact without being confrontational. For men to stay on their side of the line in a conversation, sometimes it's easier if they go walking together, golfing or driving so as to reduce the amount of direct eye contact. Conversely, not making eye contact with a woman can signal your disinterest.

Listening

Being a 40 percent listener is just as important as being a 40 percent speaker.

- ❑ How would you characterize your listening style? Can you listen and be present for five straight minutes without judging or interrupting someone?

- ❑ Do you find yourself being really attentive or perhaps thinking about something else? Is your listening clouded by prejudgment or emotional baggage?

- ❑ Do you actually listen at 40 percent, or are you just waiting for an opening so you can begin talking?

- ❑ Do you repeat what you've heard to clarify your understanding and confirm that you are listening?

❑ When you give advice, is it only after it was *asked for*?

Victim, Villain or Hero

When considering the above, be sure to ask:

❑ What kind of energy am I playing with? Is that the energy of a victim, villain or hero?

❑ Am I staying on my side of the 50 percent line in dealing with this, or am I being sucked into other people's dramas?

❑ How does the other person feel around me (victim, villain or hero)?

❑ What do their eyes, voice and body language tell me (80 percent or 20 percent)?

❑ Do they feel free to speak the truth? Is there a "safe place" to do it?

❑ Are they ready to listen? Are they in a time and place where they can give me their undivided attention?

❑ Last, since we are both good people, how can we co-create a win/win solution?

Most people find it worth learning the language of the heart, which is feelings. Here's to relating from your heart with the people you work with every day.

Note: There are additional insights and exercises and on the web site www.victimsvillainsandheroes.com.

Part IV ~ Workplace Heroes

Workplace Heroes

What follows is the experience of three people who studied with us and then applied what they learned to their careers. As you will soon find out, playing 40/40 is a powerful reference for success in your relationships both at work and at home.

Bob

Bob has successfully run an automotive repair service for more than twenty years. He employs more than twenty people, including service writers, mechanics and custodial help.

Bob shared insights into how his understanding of *The Plot* profoundly affected the way he runs his business. By moving to a 40 percent level, Bob was able to extricate himself from sixteen-hour workdays and re-focus from working "in his business" to working "on his business."

According to Bob, the single biggest change brought about by understanding *The Plot* was his being more compassionate toward his employees. He realized he and his employees were all playing roles in *The Plot*.

For the first time ever, he began talking about feelings with his employees. He said his conversations now came from the heart. As a result, the employees feel safer when communicating with him.

When technicians approached Bob in the past, it was usually at an 80 percent energy level. Being an 80 percenter himself, a win/lose discussion would immediately follow, resulting in bad feelings all around. Since Bob was the boss, you can imagine who always won. You can also imagine how a defeated 80 percenter might feel.

Bob now focuses on the emotional connection first. Bob stated that when his workers came to him with 80 percent energy in the past, he would react either by shutting them off and letting them know that he did not want to hear their problems ... or he would come right back at them with his own 80 percent energy. Now he lets them know that coming at him with 80 percent energy is too strong, which immediately softens the men. Bob says that as long as he stays at a 40 percent level, he finds that the technicians begin to wind down, often apologizing for their strong energy and then talking openly about how they feel. To quote Bob, "It is amazing how soft some of my toughest guys are."

Many star performers are moody, proud, ego-driven people by nature. Much of their success and professionalism compensate for hidden fears. In essence, they are running for their lives.

Bob shared that many of his best performers were the hardest ones to discipline. They react by being overly righteous and are impossible to correct. Star performers send out the message: "Don't mess with me because I know what I am doing."

Unfortunately, many star performers can be critical of co-workers. This is in part because, at an emotional level, they want to stay top dog by keeping other people down.

We asked Bob when he felt these star performers were most vulnerable. He stated it was when they were happy, usually at the end of a week in which they had accomplished a lot. When they had nothing left to prove, their masks could come off. They'd have a beer together and then the men would loosen up.

Bob builds teamwork with these employees by *including* them more. He now connects with his managers at a once-a-month dinner and includes rank and file workers on a rotating basis. At first they were uncomfortable with the inclusion, but eventually they opened up and began to talk about themselves and their jobs in a healing manner. It is truly incredible to watch blame and justification disappear when everyone operates at a 40 percent level.

When asked what he was trying to control these days, Bob said, "Just about nothing." He has delegated as much as possible. He no longer works ten-hour days, six days a week. He now spends his time at work focusing on developing relationships with his workers and customers—a responsibility he can execute better than anyone else.

Bob shared that his people were a lot smarter than he gave them credit for. He said they have lots of great opinions and that he has been able to grow them through inclusion. Bob acknowledged that he had an open- door policy, which had never worked until he was finally open himself. He said, "You have to make yourself accessible."

We asked Bob how he deals with a worker who doesn't perform up to expectation. He had a perfect example: a technician whom we will call Hans was caught using a harsh tone of voice with one of his customers. Hans, a precise mechanic, had the unfortunate habit of making his customers feel guilty about not taking better care of their cars.

One day Bob witnessed Hans berating a customer for not taking better care of her BMW. Rather than jump into the drama, Bob told himself, "Wow, that was interesting!" and stored it away for later in the day. When things had slowed down, Bob approached Hans and gently said, "I noticed a bit of upset on the part of Mrs. Jones today." And then Bob said nothing more. Immediately, Hans apologized, and they talked about what could be done to make sure it didn't happen a second time. It's amazing how people are willing to take on responsibility if you stay on your side of the line.

We have a suggestion for dealing with employee discipline in light of our discussion with Bob. Using the above scenario as a model, try the following expanded approach:

➤ "I'd like to discuss something with you. Where would you like to go to talk about it?" (Remember, we want to place the other person in a "safe" environmental space.)

➤ "I noticed a bit of upset on the part of Mrs. Jones today." This statement stays on Bob's side of the 50 yard line. The word "you" is not used, nor is the person's performance specifically criticized. Rather, it is an observation about someone else's discomfort. Chances are, if you say nothing more and wait, the employee will begin to acknowledge the shortcoming. If they don't, go to the next question.

➤ "Was the conversation with Mrs. Jones the type of interaction we want to have with our clients?" Again, the focus is on the activity. This may prompt the desired response on the part of the employee as it did in Hans's situation. However, if they remain defensive, move on to the next question.

➤ "How could the conversation with Mrs. Jones have been approached differently?" This narrows the inquiry. If the light bulb in their head hasn't turned on by this point, then it's time to let them know what you expect, while doing so from your side of the line.

➤ "In my opinion, this is not how we want Mrs. Jones or any other client to feel about working with us." Then wait again. And be patient. Your silence will signal that it's their time to speak up. By this time the employee ought to be realizing that any response on their part should focus not on blame or justification, but rather on taking responsibility for the situation. As long as you stay at 40 percent, the chances of the employee owning the criticism and the solution remain alive.

➤ "Lastly, let me share how I feel about this situation and what I believe should be done differently next time. Does this make sense to you? Can we agree to take this approach next time?"

When you get to the point of discussing resolution, you must come from the standpoint of *"We are two good people. We can resolve this."* It's not a bad idea to use this phrase as a mantra. It works with couples at home as well as with workplace relationships.

We continued our interview with Bob by addressing a concern shared by many business owners and managers introduced to this material: "If I weren't *driving* this business, how could I be assured it would succeed?"

This is an emotional response to some fear. It's about running for our lives. Bob quickly stated that he shared those fears, too. The breakthrough he had after going through *The Plot* training was realizing that he could accomplish more when he came from a 40 percent place. He said he was no longer on the 80/20 roller-coaster ride. He said that even though he was an 80 percenter on the outside, in many respects he was a 20 percenter emotionally.

Eighty-percent energy can be misleading. While it feels like real strength, it is based on fear, which is not a sustainable position. Real strength based on positive heart-driven energies is far more powerful and sustainable.

Bob says the most profound thing about coming from a 40 percent place is that now he is able to receive at a heart level. For the first time, he is open to praise and the warmth others have to give.

So profound was the effect that after Bob found himself injured in an automobile accident and unable to go to work for more than six weeks, his company had its best months ever! He stated that previous absences would create one big drama. He would dread going on vacation because there would be nonstop calls from clients and employees. He said the silence during the six-week span was almost deafening. It certainly was an eye-opener.

The final question we asked Bob was, "What is your deepest commitment to your work force?" Without hesitation he replied, "Learning to be at a 40 percent level with everyone." His focus today is on inclusion and empowerment. Bob's business has never been more profitable, he has never had more personal time, and he has never been happier.

Simon

Simon is a software engineer. His first story involved a manager who constantly pressured him to get work done within a very short period of time.

Simon, a conscientious worker, told his boss there was not enough time to complete a certain project properly. However, his boss responded with 80 percent emotional energy on the issue, and any concerns Simon had would fall on deaf ears. As a result, getting yelled at or a one-word response to an e-mailed concern was not uncommon.

Eventually Simon's work began to suffer, as any time he would make a suggestion he felt he had to prepare to defend himself for the forthcoming negative response. Simon began feeling and acting like a victim. ("He doesn't care about me. He's not a good person. He's a villain.")

The relationship between Simon and his boss was further strained by the fact that the company was going through a series of layoffs. Simon feared for his job, as did the other employees. This made his likelihood of speaking up even less than before. Anyone who spoke up felt they might be next in line during the layoff. As a result, communication—so critical during this period of the company's history—declined dramatically.

One day, after his experience of going through course work in *The Plot*, Simon realized that he had been a 20 percenter and needed to step up to a 40 percent level. This time he sent the following e-mail: "John, it took a bit of courage for me to send this e-mail. Over the past few months I ..." He expressed how he felt he was forced to defend himself every time they had a communication. He shared that this was affecting his attitude and productivity. Simon also said he was aware of the pressures John faced, but knew they were both good people and could work together better than this. He sent the e-mail on a Friday afternoon so that his boss would have the weekend to think about it.

And it worked. As a result of this e-mail, Simon and his boss opened a new dialogue. He found himself having a much better relationship with his boss, whose attitude seemed to have changed.

What happened? To begin with, it was clear that his boss was an 80 percenter. These people generally don't hear the first few nos, especially if they are too panicked or too strong.

Most 80 percenters want to be pushed back, but they have to be challenged with an opportunity, not threatened. Ultimately, Simon's boss welcomed his coming forward as a 40 percenter in a challenging and non-threatening manner.

Simon made an interesting comment. He stated that in order to reduce his fear of a layoff or retribution from "stepping up" to his boss, he arranged for a job interview to provide himself with an alternative. This is incredibly wise thinking on the road from 20 to 40 percent. The more choices or "outs" we give ourselves, the less likely we will play the victim role.

Many an employee has remained in their culture of silence for fear of losing a job. However, very few of them realized that this fear was mostly of their own making. The fact is you don't have to work for a jerk if you don't want to.

Simon then told another interesting story. After doing the coursework in *The Plot*, Simon began the interviewing process for another position. Because of his high-in-demand skills, he was used to companies recruiting him. In the past, he liked the attention these recruiters gave him, but his emotional nature felt more comfortable with staying put, regardless of how much he disliked his job. (Remind anyone of Dilbert?)

This time, however, he approached things differently. He began by asking himself questions like, "What do I want to do with my career?" After getting very clear about that, he then asked himself when interviewing prospective employers, "How do I think it would feel working for this company? Do they fit into my plans?" By coming from that reference point, Simon was able to attract an employer of his choice, where his opinion was respected and his efforts were rewarded.

Now that Simon has graduated from *The Plot*, he finds the joy in his work. He also gets paid more than ever. In the past he felt that he had to force himself to work. Now he goes to work and finds the "charming aspects" of what he is doing. He feels less pressure and has become more open. There was no room to do that when he was a 20 percenter coming from a fight or flight reference.

In Buddhist terms, you want to find the *dharma* in the work you do, no matter what it is. Being a 40 percenter opens you up to the spiritual side of your work life.

Simon made a final insightful comment. He stated that the dot-com community is all about "connection," yet many companies still don't "get it." He has learned that in order to move at Internet speed *we need to feel in order to connect.*

Simon has realized that being successful today is about being proactive about how you feel, not reactive. You, like Simon, have the power to choose what role you will play at work.

Holly

Holly was introduced to *The Plot* at its inception. She has a background in high-end sales to an affluent client base, including yacht and helicopter charters and time-shares for a major resort.

Holly shared that the most powerful reference she obtained from *The Plot* was the understanding that *"We are both good people and that sales is about playing 40/40."* She now focuses on building a relationship from the heart first, before coming close to discussing the subject of her sales call. Because of this approach, she believes there are many people who buy from her just because they feel good being around her, because she finds the good in them.

Holly had a story to share about her days employed selling time-shares for a major company. Year after year Holly was the top-selling agent. She had a very personable boss who was low key in his ways and basically just let her do her job.

Unfortunately, while his approach worked for Holly, it did not work for other sales agents who needed more encouragement and focus. Her boss, despite being an extremely likable man, managed from a 20 percent energy level, which was not enough to encourage, coax and inspire most of his workers.

Anxious to boost sales, the company fired her boss and in his place hired a "real mover and shaker." Apparently this fellow was not only a mover and shaker but also a person willing to "churn 'em and burn 'em" without losing any sleep over it. Holly felt he was a villainous 80 percenter as his motivational tactics were all fear-based. Any progress on the part of poor performers was born out of fear and short-lived. Most ended up terminated, and many of those who stayed ended up robbing the company blind. (Fight or flight anyone?)

It came as no surprise that the company ended up facing numerous legal difficulties due to this manager's tendency to misrepresent facts. He would promise things to employees and clients that he never followed up on. He also motivated the employees to work long hours without extra pay to make the numbers look good, an activity for which the company eventually paid dearly when it settled a number of overtime claims.

All of us have seen these managers come and go. They are part of what Don refers to as the "million-dollar executive club" and it's not because of what they get paid but instead because of the amount of damage they cause! Interestingly, these managers seldom get fired: That is that last thing they want on their resumes. After they wear out their welcome and cause their damage, they typically move on to another unsuspecting employer, continually building their squeaky clean resume in the process. Because so many employers are afraid when asked for a reference to "tell it like it is," these villainous executives usually escape without repercussion.

Why are these people hired in the first place? It's due in part to the employers' own fears. They rush to judgment because of their desperate needs, not because something necessarily feels right. If you feel someone has a strong energy, it is important to ask, "What techniques do you employ to include others?" "How do you manage poor performing employees?" And, of course, "Tell me about something in your last job that felt unfair."

The typical mover and shaker will seek out a sales incentive system that rewards only the top performer. That person will get a trip to Hawaii every year while everyone else is left behind. The problem with the "one winner and the rest losers" approach is that very little information gets shared. There is no incentive for the top performer to become inclusive—which creates a system that encourages villainous behavior and generates needless drama.

Holly has been successful selling high-ticket items to affluent customers because she views them as human beings first. She says that rich people are human and have relationship needs like anyone else. Unlike many people, she is not intimidated by people who have money. She does not get caught up in whether she is accepted or rejected by them. She does not play a more-than/less-than game.

She is aware that many affluent clients are concerned about other people trying to use them. She is very concerned that many sales techniques tend toward the manipulative, which is villainous in its nature. She believes that sales as a numbers game falls into *The Plot*, whereas sales as a relationship-building exercise does not.

Again, many successful and affluent people are 80 percenters because they are frightened and running for their lives. They fear what may happen if they stop and feel in the present moment. As Holly discovered, you can slow them down from their 80 percent energy by touching them at a personal level and making a heart-to-heart connection.

Conclusion

It is time to draw the curtain on the show *Goodness Triumphs Over Evil*. As the world's longest-running drama, it greatly affects the joy and prosperity of our working lives. We can be grateful it is no longer required for our personal or organizational growth. Ideas that once made a lot of sense cause plenty of harm when they outlive their purpose. The good old show falls into this category.

You can create a company or career of joy, fun and bliss for yourself and others. Today. Now. In the present moment. Participating in *The Plot* will never get you there, as love and laughter were never part of its script. The aim of that drama was to increase your strength and your cleverness, with just a short break between the performances.

Don't wait for the show to close—run offstage to the nearest exit now! Why would you want to become a victim to suffer more? Why would you want to be a villain to yourself or another? Why would you want to feel unfairness, blame and arrogance? Why would you ever want to work for or with a villain? Even being a negative hero, trying too hard to save other victims results in "compassion fatigue" and starts losing its luster after a while.

Why would you want to languish in a poor relationship to be rewarded at the end with just a tiny morsel of love, when you have so much love in your own heart? Or run a business or work in a job that doesn't call to your heart when you have so much to offer?

Start studying your new script, with its stage directions of emotional heart space. It won't be long before you'll be living in your heart, not letting unconscious drama and conflict lure you out to play. You'll find your heart brimming over with creativity as your career unfolds.

Your greatest role will begin when you step onto your own stage of life as a conscious creator. This is when the real fun begins at work. You make money from what calls to you. No longer are you dependent on someone else's energy. You have your own as you create business magic!

Our new play is called *As You Like It,* and it's by you, not Shakespeare. We'll look for you under the stars!

Summary: How to Become Your Own Hero

VICTIM → HERO

- ❑ Move from 20 to 40 percent emotional energy.

- ❑ Become 100 percent responsible.

- ❑ Don't blame, justify or criticize.

- ❑ Don't focus on your "rights" or "entitlements ," instead focus on your responsibilities and opportunities.

- ❑ Coax, encourage and inspire yourself.

- ❑ Educate yourself. Get information.

- ❑ Take the first step. See how it feels.

- ❑ Get support.

- ❑ Embrace your mistakes. Learn from them.

- ❑ What is the FEAR?

- ❑ Look for the familiar experience.

- ❑ Start journaling, walking, exercising.

- ❑ Reward your efforts.

- ❑ _____

VILLAIN → HERO

- ❑ Move from 80 to 40 percent emotional energy.

- ❑ Disengage, e.g., "Wow, That's Interesting!"

- ❑ Sit down, breathe, walk, "take five."

- ❑ Get clear about the source of the pain..

- ❑ Identify the prior experience.

- ❑ Attack the conduct, not the person.

- ❑ Don't justify hurting others.

- ❑ Think about the long-term consequences of your actions.

- ❑ Get your drama outside of work and home.

- ❑ Don't abuse, control or manipulate.

- ❑ Don't "vomit" on people by yelling at them.

- ❑ Focus on what is good about you.

- ❑ Get professional help.

- ❑ _____

BECOMING YOUR OWN HERO

NEGATIVE HERO → HERO

- ☐ Move from 80 to 40 percent emotional energy.

- ☐ Stop running! Be present.

- ☐ Ask how you feel.

- ☐ Ask how they must feel.

- ☐ Then be inclusive of those feelings.

- ☐ Quit beating yourself up.

- ☐ Use "I" words, not "you' words.

- ☐ Engage in active listening.

- ☐ Don't try to solve all the problems.

- ☐ Don't over-commit.

- ☐ Give up the need to control.

- ☐ Feel loving and accept love from others.

- ☐ Encourage, coax and inspire victims.

- ☐ Manage by Agreement.

- ☐ _____

These checklists can be found on the Web site at www.victimsvillainsheroes.com in pocket size so you can easily carry them around in your wallet or purse.

Feeling Your Way Through The Plot

Use this worksheet to recognize and resolve Plot scenarios. [It includes an example given to us by one of Don's coaching clients in *italics*.] Remember that the emotions are drawn to stories and drama,

1. Lets give this drama a name: [*i.e. Me and My Business Partner*]

_____

_____

_____

2. What is the stage you are on? (Describe the physical and factual setting.) [*The worst is in group meetings either at the office or with a client.*]

_____

_____

_____

_____

_____

3. Who are all the players on this stage?   *[Me, Tony, the executive team, and sometimes clients.]*

_____

_____

_____

_____

_____

4. What feels unfair? What drives you crazy?
[Tony dominates the meetings. Even though I own half the company, I can't seem to get a word in anywhere. Many times he says things I don't agree with.]

_____

_____

_____

_____

_____

_____

_____

5. Why does this feel unfair? Why does it drive you crazy? [*Because some of what he says is flat out wrong or not what we agreed to. Drives me crazy because we are losing key executives and clients over it.*]

_____

_____

_____

_____

_____

_____

6. How does this drama make your "circle of influence" feel? (Include co-workers, clients, family and friends.) [*I think many of our executives are embarrassed about it. Others ask me what I'm going to do about it.*]

_____

_____

_____

_____

_____

7. How does this drama affect the "bigger picture"? (Company culture, your career, world peace.) [It could affect the company. My career and my pocketbook. I haven't figured out the world peace part yet.]

_____

_____

_____

_____

_____

8. What is the "good" you think any villain or negative hero in this drama is seeking? (Remember, they are trying to move from pain toward pleasure, even if their methods and outcomes are less than desirable.) [I do think his intentions are good, but I'm not so sure anymore. I know he wants more sales just like I do.]

_____

_____

_____

_____

_____

9. How strong is your energy in this situation? Is it over 40%? Is this an emergency? Is it under 40%? Are you throwing a pity party? *[I'm clearly the 20 percenter. It really feels unfair.]*

_____

_____

_____

_____

10. What mannerisms and tone of voice do you use when acting out this drama? Either *act out* this behavior in front of a mirror or another person, or write out your feelings below.
[Problem is I don't do much. Anytime I have spoken up, I get such a strong response back it's not worth dealing with it. Kinda like dealing with my teenage daughter!]

_____

_____

_____

_____

_____

_____

11. What role does that leave you playing? Victim? Negative hero? Villain? If you are not trying to triumph over this, have you given up? If so, is it because you are playing a victim role or because you have completely walked off the stage? *[Definitely the victim. I haven't given up completely. We still have a good thing going and I don't want to mess that up.]*

----

12. What is the better way to meet everyone's emotional needs? *[I have to begin doing a better job of speaking up for myself. I can acknowledge that he is trying his best, too. Perhaps a third party can bring us closer to the table. Even better, maybe we go on a long walk or hike together.]*

----

13. What is the good in this drama? Why do you need this? What can it help you learn? Why would God have had you go through this situation? (For example: "To give up arrogance and learn humility.") [*I've always had challenges dealing with people who have a strong energy. This can help me learn how to be my own hero. If we can't get to a 40/40, I will have to consider letting go.*]

_____

_____

_____

_____

14. What are you going to do about this to end the drama? [*Start by inviting him to go on a weekend retreat. Just him and me away from it all. We can both let down our defenses and talk man to man.*]

_____

_____

_____

The Plot Poem

The timeless drama continues;
The Plot takes center stage.
"Goodness Triumphs Over Evil,"
emotions leading the way.

Victim, villain and hero: we play all the
parts,
blaming and justifying, breaking each others'
hearts,
playing roles we don't quite understand,
letting stories from the past ruin our perfect
plans.

Let's tear off these masks
and run out the stage door!
We don't need this drama
to learn our lessons anymore!

Also by Don Phin

Don spent years representing workplace victims against their villainous bosses (at least that's what he thought he was doing). Older and wiser, Don now focuses on eliminating unwanted drama from the workplace. His books and materials have helped thousands of business owners, managers and employees prevent destructive employee lawsuits while building powerful relationships and growing the bottom-line.

Don is a national workshop leader and consultant, as well as president of the Employer Advisors Network, Inc. He designed the *HR That Works* series of personnel management and compliance products and is the author of numerous books and articles, including *LAWSUIT FREE! How to Prevent Employee Lawsuits* and *Building Powerful Employment Relationships!* Don believes compliance struggles simply mirror the difficulty we have in establishing any relationship, including the one with ourselves.

To see Don's vision for the workplace, go to www.donphin.com/vision.asp

For more information on these books and additional services, please visit our Web sites:

www.DonPhin.com
www.HRThatWorks.net
www.VictimsVillainsandHeroes.com
Coming soon: www.PurpleHR.com
(it may already be here by the time you read this)

Also by Loy Young

Adventure. . .what is it to you?
Racing around the track in an F1 Ferrari?
Heli-skiing in the Alps?
Sailing single-handedly around the globe?
Bare-handed bull-wrestling?
Orbiting the earth in a NASA capsule?

The ultimate adventure for Loy Young has been seeking understanding of our human behavior. In spite of our high spiritual ideals, religious teachings and incredible scientific advancements, she feels there has been little change in human behavior since Cain and Abel. Why? She's always wanted to know.

A mystery Loy felt compelled to unravel, she was willing to travel into the depths of darkness of our human consciousness. This might sound far too serious, no fun at all to most people, but it's pure excitement to Loy, her destiny to fulfill.

This conscious quest has taken more than four decades and spanned six continents, interacting with people from all walks of life—from cosmopolitan jet-setters to rural villagers—and a variety of cultural backgrounds and religions. Whenever she found an answer that has proven to be beneficial, she has written and spoken about it, taught classes, and used it in counseling with those who sought valuable advice. Some of it has turned out to be only partial truths, sending her on her way once again, to search for more complete truths.

It has often been a perilous journey with Loy nearly drowning in the sea of opposites many times. The search has not been in vain though; she feels she has found the answers she was seeking.

Loy says she felt like Newton must have felt when he discovered gravity, it had always been with us, but it took him being hit over the head with an apple, before he had his "ah ha." Only then were we able to make use of a natural phenomenon which then helped us advance greatly scientifically. Loy says she had to be hit on the head for thousands of hours listening to people's life stories before she recognized it. "Ah ha, that's the natural phenomenon all humans experience." Finally she understood why there had been little change in human behavior since the dawn of humanity. The answers for permanent change lie in our feelings, not our mind.

Since her discovery, Loy has co-authored a series of books about these findings hoping to indeed help us advance greatly with our human behavior. First in 1994, she co-authored a book entitled *The Script of Life* with her long time research partner, Robert F. Young to help individuals awaken to their feelings and the roles they unconsciously play over and over, preventing lasting change. Four years later, in 1998, after testing out her theories with people in personal relationships in a wide variety of cultures, she wrote *The Plot: Dealing with*

Feelings, Victims, Villains and Heroines. That book was the starting point for this book co-authored with Don Phin.

You're invited to learn more about Loy's work by visiting her Web site *www.LoyYoung.com.*

Illustrated by
Francine Dufour

Francine is a multifaceted artist whose work spans the range from classical oil painting to exuberant silk painting to electronic art and Web design. View Francine's art on her Web site:

www.SilkPaintingGallery.com

Edited and Produced
by Kathryn Hall and
Karen Risch

Kathryn has worked in many roles within the publishing industry during the past 20 years—as an author, editor, production manager and, most recently, as a project manager for Web sites.

Karen has been a professional writer and editor since the early 1980s. A collaborator and contributor to several bestsellers, she is drawn to edit meaningful projects that offer innovative resources for people to better their lives. Learn more about her literary and editorial services by visiting www.JustWriteNow.com